FUTILITY CLOSET

FUTILITY CLOSET

An Idler's Miscellany of Compendious Amusements

by GREG ROSS

FUTILITY CLOSET BOOKS

Raleigh, North Carolina

CONTENTS

PREFACE

In November 2002, shortly after becoming an editor at *American Scientist* magazine, I started a personal blog. Like a lot of blogs, it was just a collection of my own observations and opinions about current events and life in general. After 20 years as a magazine editor, I enjoyed the freedom of writing spontaneously, but it began to feel rather self-important. Who cares what *I* think about things?

I liked the business of running a blog, though, so I cast about for something else to write about. Years earlier I had come across O. Henry's dictum *Write what you like, there is no other rule.* "I'll give you the whole secret of short story writing, and here it is," he had said. "Rule one, write stories that please yourself. There is no rule two. If you can't write a story that pleases yourself, you'll never please the public."

I wasn't writing fiction, but I had always wondered whether this advice might apply to any sort of writing, and the blog seemed a painless way to try it out. So I tried to imagine the website that I myself would most like to read, one that seemed tailor-made to my own predilections, without regard to a larger audience. Such a site would be updated regularly, and it would cover the topics that interest me personally—language, literature, history, mathematics, quotations, puzzles, art, philosophy, and curiosities of all kinds. And it would present each item as concisely as possible, so that whether I had an hour to spend or only a minute, I could come away feeling that my visit had been worthwhile.

I remember writing a test post about Antarctica, just to see what this would look like. It seemed workable, so I began writing posts.

That's basically it. In trying to realize this vision over the ensuing eight years I've published more than 7,000 items, plundering first my memory, then my files, then my bookshelf, then local public libraries, and finally the three big universities of North Carolina's Research Triangle: Duke University in Durham, the University of North Carolina in Chapel Hill, and North Carolina State University in Raleigh. But I've always written to please myself, trusting O. Henry that if I did this faithfully then like-minded readers might find some value in it.

He was right. Though I've never publicized it, Futility Closet has grown steadily year after year. As I write this, in August 2013, the site has served 67 million pageviews to 22 million unique visitors.

While all this enterprise has generated an archive of interesting material, from my perspective it's essentially been an exercise in library research. In a given month I visit all three university campuses, swimming through the big main libraries and smaller specialty libraries in art, law, medicine, design, music, science, and divinity. I'm also continuously ransacking the Triangle's three public library systems, and I order rarer books by interlibrary loan.

What I'm doing on these trips is a combination of lead-chasing, fact-checking, and serendipitous prospecting. The great glory of a university library is that you can pursue absolutely anything— on my shelf as I write this are books on Apollo 11, the history of cannibalism, the philosophy of madness, premodern Japanese poetry, eccentric architecture, the fourth dimension, and coincidences between twins. Any one of these might spark an idea that I can confirm elsewhere, opening more avenues to further books and generating posts for the site as I go.

There is no point or purpose to any of this; I'm just following my nose. Given the name Futility Closet, a number of readers have inferred, understandably, that the site is essentially about futility, and interpret the posts in that light. I don't conceive it that way, but I certainly am attracted to human foibles and failings, and I imagine this comes across in the writing, so that interpretation isn't really wrong.

(In fact the name's origin is more mundane. In the mid-1990s my wife was a graduate student at American University in Washington D.C. One day while visiting the campus with her I noticed that someone had scratched an F into a door marked UTILITY CLOSET. Somehow this stuck in my head, and years later, when I was searching for a domain name, futilitycloset.com was one of the few candidates I could think of that was still available.)

This book collects some of my favorite finds in eight years of research. (There are mountains more, which I hope to share in future books.) Like the website, it's a miscellany, with no organization, no theme, and no point. You can read the book straight through if you like, or backward, or dip into it at random. Each item stands on its own. While there's no room to list all the sources I've consulted, I've tried to give enough information that interested readers can pursue chosen topics on their own. I hope you enjoy reading the book as much as I've enjoyed compiling it.

I must thank the readers, whose intelligence, patience, and good humor have made this whole project a continuing joy to work on. I owe particular thanks also to Gary Antonick, Mark Frauenfelder, Mark Heath, Lucian Marin, Chris Merritt, Greg Mortimer, John Ross, Lee Sallows, Daniel Summers, and every librarian in North Carolina. Final and deepest thanks go to my wife, Sharon, whose unfailing support and bewildering love would have led me to succeed in anything.

PART ONE

BLACKMAIL, LIGHTNING, and THE EARL of LEICESTER

FIRST CLASS

On April 17, 1944, Howard Hughes flew a Lockheed Constellation from California to Washington, D.C., in just under seven hours.

On the way back he picked up Orville Wright in Ohio, giving him the last airplane flight of his life.

The Constellation's wingspan, 126 feet, was 6 feet greater than the length of Wright's first flight in 1903.

• • •

ELSEWHERE

Notable cross-references in the index of Donald Tovey's *Essays in Musical Analysis, Volume VI*, 1939:

> Agnostic, *see* Dachsund.
> Appendicitis, *see* Cadenza.
> Critics, *see* Experts.
> Experts, *see* Critics.
> Giraffe, *see* Berlioz.
> Hedgehog, *see* Brahms.
> Monster, *see* Loch Ness.
> Noodles, *see* Brahms on plagiarism.
> Pope, *see* Bruckner.
> Sneeze, *see* Cherubini and Beethoven.
> Sugar, *see* Grocer.
> Witchery, *see* Mendelssohn.

Evelyn Waugh owned a translation of Tolstoy's novel *Resurrection* for which someone had composed "a particularly felicitous index. The first entry is: 'Adultery, 13, 53, 68, 70'; the last is 'Why do people punish? 358'. Between them occur such items as: Cannibalism, Dogs, Good breeding, Justification of one's position, Seduction, Smoking, Spies, and Vegetarianism."

• • •

NEVER MIND

During an Air Force training mission over Montana on Feb. 2, 1970, Gary Foust's F-106 entered an uncontrollable flat spin at 35,000 feet.

He rode it down to 12,000 feet, ejected—and watched as the plane righted itself, descended into a snowy field, and made a gentle belly landing. Its engine was still running when the police arrived.

After repairs, the fighter was returned to service in California and New York. Today it's on display in a museum at Wright-Patterson Air Force Base in Ohio.

• • •

THE BERNERS STREET HOAX

In 1810, Theodore Hook, a writer of comic operas, bet his friend Samuel Beazley that he could turn any house in London into the most talked-about address in the city within one week. Beazley accepted, and Hook began writing letters.

A few weeks later, on Nov. 10, a Mrs. Tottenham of 54 Berners Street turned away a coal merchant delivering a load of coal that she hadn't ordered.

She was in for a long day. The *Morning Post* reported: "Wagons laden with coals from the Paddington wharfs, upholsterers' goods in cart loads, organs, pianofortes, linens, jewelry, and every other description of furniture sufficient to have stocked the whole street, were lodged as near as possible to the door of 54, with anxious trades-people and a laughing mob."

It went on. "There were accoucheurs, tooth-drawers, miniature painters, artists of every description, auctioneers, . . .grocers, mercers, post-chaises, mourning-coaches, poultry, rabbits, pigeons, etc. In fact, the whole street was literally filled with the motley group."

The merchants were followed by dignitaries: the governor of the Bank of England, the archbishop of Canterbury, cabinet ministers, dukes, and finally the lord mayor of London.

Hook won his bet, collecting one guinea. He eventually confessed to the prank, but apparently never received any punishment.

• • •

TRUTHFUL NUMBERS

- FOUR contains four letters.
- TEN is spelled with ten raised dots in Braille.
- TWELVE is worth 12 points in Scrabble.
- FIFTEEN is spelled with 15 dots and dashes in International Morse Code.

TWENTY-NINE contains 29 straight lines—if you don't count the hyphen.

• • •

THE BLACKMAIL PARADOX

It's legal for me to expose your infidelity.

And it's legal for me to seek $10,000 from you in a business transaction.

So why is it illegal for me to blackmail you for $10,000?

"Most crimes do not need theories to explain why the behavior is criminal," writes Northwestern law professor James Lindgren. "The wrongdoing is self-evident. But blackmail is unique among major crimes: no one has yet figured out why it ought to be illegal."

• • •

THE KRUSKAL COUNT

Here's a card trick devised by Rutgers physicist Martin Kruskal. Give a friend a deck of cards and ask her to follow these instructions:

1. Think of a "secret number" from 1 to 10. (Example: 6)

2. Shuffle the deck and deal the cards face up one at a time, counting silently as you go.

3. When you reach the secret number, note the value of that card and adopt it as your new secret number. Aces count as 1; face cards count as 5. (Example: If the 6th card is a 4, then 4 becomes your new secret number.)

4. Continue dealing, counting silently anew from 1 each time you adopt a new number. Remember the last secret card you reach.

That's it. You just stand there and watch her deal. When she's finished, you can identify her final secret card in any way you please, preferably through a grotesquely extortionate wager.

You can do this because you've simply played along. When she's dealing, note the value of an early card and then silently follow the same steps that she is. Five times out of six, your "paths" through the deck will intersect and your final secret card will match hers. That's far from obvious, though; the trick can be baffling if you refuse to explain it.

• • •

STEAMPUNK CHAUFFER

Zadoc Dederick and Isaac Grass quietly patented this as an "improvement in steam-carriage" in 1868, but the details are pretty sensational: They'd invented a mechanical man with jointed legs who could pull a cart, lift its legs to clear obstacles, and even run backward.

The boiler is in the torso. "It is unnecessary to describe this part of the mechanism, as there is nothing peculiar in it."

• • •

OUT WITH A BANG

Lawyer James Otis was a hero in American politics before the revolution. In his later years he used to tell his sister, "I hope, when God Almighty in his righteous providence shall take me out of time into eternity, that it will be by a flash of lightning."

On May 23, 1783, he was standing in a doorway during a thundershower, telling a story to his family, when his wish came true.

"No mark of any kind could be found on Otis," ran one account of his death, "nor was there the slightest change or convulsion on his features."

"This flash of lightning was the first that came from the cloud, and was not followed by any others that were remarkable."

• • •

OH

Harvard philosopher Willard Van Orman Quine typed all his work on an old 1927 Remington typewriter. He had customized it by replacing the 1, !, and ? keys with specialized mathematical symbols.

Someone once asked him how he managed to write without using a question mark.

"Well, you see," he replied, "I deal in certainties."

• • •

APT

In Pig Latin, TRASH becomes ASHTRAY.

• • •

AN ALARMING PARADOX

In 1735, an anonymous "lover of mathematicks" offered the following conundrum:

"'Tis certainly Matter of Fact, that three certain Travellers went on a Journey, in which, tho' their Heads travelled full twelve Yards more than their Feet, yet they all return'd alive, with their Heads on."

How is this possible?

(See Answers and Solutions)

• • •

SHORT SUBJECTS

While adapting *The Big Sleep* for the screen, a confused Howard Hawks wired Raymond Chandler asking who was supposed to have killed General Sternwood's chauffer in the novel. Chandler responded:

NO IDEA

When a Paris news editor asked Ernest Hemingway for an accounting of his expenses, he cabled:

SUGGEST YOU UPSTICK BOOKS ASSWARDS

A movie studio once approached Eugene O'Neill to write a screenplay for a Jean Harlow film. They asked him to reply in a collect telegram of no more than 20 words. He wrote:

NO NO NO NO NO NO NO NO NO NO NO NO NO NO
NO NO NO NO O'NEILL

When Samuel Beckett won the Nobel Prize in in 1969, he received a telegram from a Parisian named Georges Godot. . . apologizing for keeping him waiting.

• • •

MISTAKEN IDENTITY

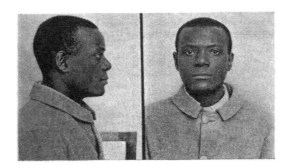

In 1903, a prisoner named Will West arrived at Leavenworth. The record clerk took the photographs above and, thinking he remembered West, asked whether he had been there before. West said no.

The clerk took some measurements, went to the file, and produced this record, bearing the name William West:

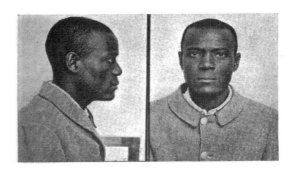

Amazed, the prisoner said, "That's my picture, but I don't know where you got it, for I know I have never been here before."

Incredibly, this was true. A different William West had been serving a life sentence at Leavenworth since 1901, and the new prisoner had the same name, face, and measurements.

The case became a strong argument in favor of the new science of fingerprinting.

• • •

NOTHING DOING

In 1873, Lewis Carroll borrowed the travel diary of his child-friend Ella Monier-Williams, with the understanding that he would show it to no one. He returned it with this letter:

 My dear Ella,

I return your book with many thanks; you will be wondering why I kept it so long. I understand, from what you said about it, that you have no idea of publishing any of it yourself, and hope you will not be annoyed at my sending three short chapters of extracts from it, to be published in *The Monthly Packet*. I have not given any names in full, nor put any more definite title to it than simply 'Ella's Diary, or The Experiences of an Oxford Professor's Daughter, during a Month of Foreign Travel.'

I will faithfully hand over to you any money I may receive on account of it, from Miss Yonge, the editor of *The Monthly Packet*.

Your affect. friend,
C.L. Dodgson

Ella thought he was joking, and wrote to tell him so, but he replied:

I grieve to tell you that every word of my letter was strictly true. I will now tell you more—that Miss Yonge has not declined the MS., but she will not give more than a guinea a chapter. Will that be enough?

"This second letter succeeded in taking me in," Ella later recalled, "and with childish pleasure I wrote and said I did not quite understand how it was my journal could be worth printing, but expressed my pleasure. I then received this letter:—"

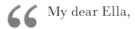 My dear Ella,

I'm afraid I have hoaxed you too much. But it really was true. I 'hoped you wouldn't be annoyed at my etc.' for the very good reason that I hadn't done it. And I gave no other title than 'Ella's Diary,' nor did I give that title. Miss Yonge hasn't declined it—because she hasn't seen it. And I need hardly explain that she hasn't given more than three guineas!
Not for three hundred guineas would I have shown it to any one—after I had promised you I wouldn't.

In haste,
Yours affectionately,
C.L.D.

• • •

APPLIED MATH

Each term in the Fibonacci sequence is derived by adding the two preceding terms:

0, 1, 1, 2, 3, 5, 8, 13, 21 ...

Remarkably, you can use successive terms to convert miles to kilometers:

8 miles ≈ 13 kilometers
13 miles ≈ 21 kilometers

This works because the two units stand in the golden ratio (to within 0.5 percent).

• • •

THE RIGHT MOMENT

The second Earl of Leicester sat in Parliament for 67 years without saying a word.

His son, the third earl, was silent for 32 years.

His grandson, the fourth earl, said nothing for 23 years.

His great-grandson, the fifth earl, Thomas William Edward Coke, kept his silence for 22 years, then in 1972 rose and said, "I hope we shall use safer chemicals in place of those which have devastated the countryside."

"My record of silence is not all that remarkable because I know that my family have not been overtalkative in this house," he said later.

• • •

SMALL PRESS

The first eyewitness account of the Wright brothers' flying machine appeared in the journal *Gleanings in Bee Culture.*

The editor, beekeeper Amos I. Root, had visited the Wrights in 1904 at Huffman Prairie, Ohio, where they were working to perfect the machine after its historic first flight the preceding December.

Root sent copies of his article to *Scientific American*—but they were dismissed.

• • •

A BAD MORNING

On March 14, 1887, Rhode Island evangelist Ansel Bourne woke up in an unfamiliar room. To his astonishment, he found that he was in Norristown, Pa., where he had been running a stationery and confectioner's shop for two months, calling himself A.J. Brown.

His nephew helped him return to Providence, where psychologists diagnosed a case of dissociative fugue, multiple personality, and amnesia.

Inspired, Robert Ludlum borrowed the preacher's surname for his novel *The Bourne Identity.*

• • •

NEXT STOP

" A woman proceeding by the elevated railroad, by the side of the Niagara Falls, asked the engine-driver, 'If the rope broke, where she would go to?' The driver told her that 'If one broke they would have the other one to hold them.' The woman then said, 'Well, driver, if that broke, where should I go to?' 'Well,' said the driver, 'it just depends upon what sort of a life you have led.'

— *Tit-Bits From All the Most Interesting Books, Periodicals and Newspapers in the World,* Dec. 3, 1881

• • •

ALL GOD'S CREATURES

Ernest Thompson Seton (1860-1946) loved nature and loved God—so in a 1907 book he tried to prove that animals follow the 10 commandments:

• Thou shalt not steal: "A stick found in the woods is the property of the Rook that discovers it, and doubly his when he has labored to bring it to his nest. This is recognized law."

• Thou shalt not kill: "New born Rattlesnakes will strike instantly at a stranger of any other species, but never at one of their own."

• Honor thy father and mother: "A Hen sets out with her Chickens a-foraging; one loiters, does not hasten up at her 'cluck cluck' of invitation and command; consequently he gets lost and dies."

• Thou shalt not commit adultery: "'The promiscuous animals to-day—the Northwestern Rabbit and the Voles—are high in the scale of fecundity, low in the scale of general development, and are periodically scourged by epidemic plagues."

• Thou shalt not bear false witness: "Oftentimes a very young Hound will jump at a conclusion, think, or hope, he has the trail, then allowing his enthusiasm to carry him away, give the first tongue, shouting in Hound language, 'Trail!' The other Hounds run to this, but if a careful examination shows that he was wrong, the announcer suffers in the opinion of the pack, and after a few such blunders, that individual is entirely discredited."

- Thou shalt not covet: "A Hen had made a nest in a certain place, and was already sitting. Later another Hen, desiring the same nest, took possession several times during the owner's brief absence, adding some of her own eggs, and endeavoring to sit. The result was a state of war, and the eggs of both Hens were destroyed."

Actually, he runs out of gas here—Seton was unable to convince even himself that animals avoid making graven images, swearing, or working on Sunday. So he concludes *The Natural History of the Ten Commandments* by deciding that "Man is concerned with all" the commandments, "the animals only with the last six."

• • •

A RIDDLE

At a Cambridge dinner, Arthur C. Clarke asked Clive Sinclair, "What was the first human artifact to break the sound barrier?" What was it?

(See Answers and Solutions)

• • •

UNQUOTE

"Patriotism is your conviction that this country is superior to all other countries because you were born in it."

—George Bernard Shaw

• • •

THE WAR AHEAD

H.G. Wells' 1914 novel *The World Set Free* is not his best known, but it's certainly his most prescient—he predicted nuclear weapons:

 She felt torn out of the world. There was nothing else in the world but a crimson-purple glare and sound, deafening, all-embracing, continuing sound. Every other light had gone out about her, and against this glare hung slanting walls, pirouetting pillars, projecting fragments of cornices, and a disorderly flight of huge angular sheets of glass.

The novel imagines an invention that accelerates radioactive decay, producing unthinkably powerful bombs. (Wells even dedicated the novel "to Frederick Soddy's interpretation of radium.")

This application was far ahead of the science of the time—physicist Leó Szilárd later said it helped inspire his own conception of a nuclear chain reaction.

If that's not impressive enough: In Wells' novel, allies drop an atomic bomb on Germany during a world war in the 1940s!

• • •

A PARABLE

Ernie and Bert are fishing. "I'll bet you a dollar," says Ernie, "that if you give me two dollars I'll give you three dollars."

Bert agrees and gives Ernie two dollars. Ernie says, "I lose," returns one dollar and pockets the other.

Ernie goes on to found a successful software company and Bert dies a bitter alcoholic.

· · ·

MAILBAG

 To the Editor of the *Herald*:

I am anxious to find out the way to figure the temperature from centigrade to Fahrenheit and vice versa. In other words, I want to know, whenever I see the temperature designated on the centigrade thermometer, how to find out what it would be on Fahrenheit's thermometer.

Old Philadelphia Lady
Paris, December 24, 1899

That's reasonable enough, right? It ran in the Paris *Herald* on Dec. 27, 1899.

The curious thing is that it also ran on Dec. 28, and Dec. 29 . . .and every day thereafter for *18 years*, a total of 6,718 times.

Publisher James Gordon Bennett never gave a reason—he only told colleague James B. Townsend that "just so long as there was an average income of jocose but more often indignant and abusive letters about this letter at the Paris *Herald* office he would continue to publish it."

· · ·

IN A WORD

acersecomic
n. a person whose hair has never been cut

musophobist
n. one who regards poetry with suspicious dislike

petrichor
n. the pleasant smell accompanying the first rain after a dry spell

dromaeognathous
adj. having a palate like an emu

• • •

PLEASE STAND BY

On Oct. 15, 1910, the airship *America* took off from Atlantic City in a bid to cross the Atlantic. The six crewmembers took along a cat, Kiddo, for luck.

The frightened tabby was still underfoot when chief engineer

Melvin Vaniman tried to send a historic wireless message back to shore. So officially the first radio communication ever made from an airship in flight was:

"Roy, come and get this goddamn cat."

• • •

LESS IS MORE

As part of a modern dance program, Paul Taylor once stood motionless on stage for four minutes.

For its review, *Dance Observer* magazine ran four inches of white space.

• • •

EVEN STEVEN

❝ A Scholar traveyling, and having noe money, call'd at an Alehouse, and ask'd for a penny loafe, then gave his hostesse it againe, for a pot of ale; and having drunke it off, was going away. The woman demanded a penny of him. For what? saies he. Shee answers, for ye ale. Quoth hee, I gave you ye loafe for it. Then, said she, pay for ye loafe. Quoth hee, had you it not againe? which put ye woman to a non plus, that ye scholar went free away.

— John Ashton, *Humour, Wit, & Satire of the Seventeenth Century*, 1883

• • •

RIMSHOT

This guy takes a gorilla out golfing. At the first tee the gorilla says, "So what am I supposed to do?" The guy says, "You see that green area about 400 yards from here? You're supposed to hit the ball onto that." So the gorilla takes a club and whacks the ball and it soars up into the sky and drops down neatly on the green. The guy tees off and gets about 150 yards, so he hits an iron shot and then another iron shot and finally they arrive at the green. The gorilla says, "What do I do now?" The guy says, "Now you hit it into that cup." The gorilla says, "Why didn't you tell me that back there?"

• • •

REJECTED

In 1989, Jules Verne's great-grandson opened a disused family safe and found a forgotten manuscript. Composed in 1863, *Paris in the Twentieth Century* imagines the remote future of August 1960—a world illuminated by electric lights in which people drive horseless carriages powered by internal combustion and ride in automatic, driverless trains.

In Verne's vision, the citizens of Paris use copiers, calculators, and fax machines; inhabit skyscrapers equipped with elevators and television; and execute their criminals in electric chairs. Twenty-six years before the Eiffel Tower was erected, Verne described "an electric lighthouse, no longer much used, [that] rose into the sky to a height of 152 meters. This was the highest monument in the world, and its lights could be seen, forty leagues away, from the towers of Rouen Cathedral."

Verne's publisher had returned the manuscript because he found it too dark—in addition to the city's technological wonders, it describes overcrowding, pollution, the dissolution of social institutions, and "machines advantageously replacing human hands."

"No one today," he had written, "will believe your prophecy."

• • •

CLINICIAN, HEAL THYSELF

In *The Elements of Style*, his popular guide for writers, William Strunk declares:

"The subject of a sentence and the principal verb should not, as a rule, be separated by a phrase or clause that can be transferred to the beginning."

• • •

A CONFEDERACY OF SQUARES

When asked his age, mathematician Augustus De Morgan used to offer a clue: "I was x years of age in the year x^2." (He was 43 in 1849.)

That quirk puts De Morgan in a pretty exclusive club. Other members include Charles Atlas (who was 44 in 1936) and Jake Gyllenhaal (who will be 45 in 2025). Next up: Babies born in 2070 will be 46 in 2116.

• • •

CAPSULE SUMMARY

On May 17, 1817, Samuel Jessup died. That was bad news for his apothecary, who had been suing him over an unpaid bill—over the course of 21 years, Jessup had taken 226,934 pills, an average of 10,806 a year. Between 1812 and 1816 he took 78 pills a day, 51,590 in 1814 alone. With the addition of 40,000 bottles of mixture, juleps, and electuaries, the druggist's bill filled 55 closely written columns.

Despite all this—or perhaps because of it—Jessup lived to age 65.

• • •

CLUTCH CARGO

Prove that the number of people who shake hands an odd number of times at the opera next Thursday will be even.

(See Answers and Solutions)

• • •

DOES THIS COUNT AS PLAGIARISM?

Published in 1838, Edgar Allan Poe's novel *The Narrative of Arthur Gordon Pym of Nantucket* tells of four men who survive a shipwreck. Starving, they draw lots to see which one is to be eaten. The loser is a man named Richard Parker.

Forty-six years later, in 1884, a yacht named the *Mignonette* sank during a journey from England to Australia. Four survivors were stranded in a dinghy. After 16 days, Captain Dudley and his two mates killed and ate the cabin boy—whose name was Richard Parker.

The three eventually returned to England, where they were convicted of murder.

•••

CHILD CUSTODY

66 Here is a curious old story that is something like a puzzle: A crocodile stole a baby, 'in the days when animals could talk,' and was about to make a dinner of it. The poor mother begged piteously for her child. 'Tell me one truth,' said the crocodile, 'and you shall have your baby again.' The mother thought it over, and at last said: 'You will not give it back.' 'Is that the truth you mean to tell?' asked the crocodile. 'Yes,' replied the mother. 'Then by our agreement I keep him,' added the crocodile; 'for if you told the truth I am not going to give him back, and if it is a falsehood, then I have also won.' Said she: 'No, you are wrong. If I told the truth you are bound by your promise; and, if a falsehood, it is not a falsehood, until after you have given me my child.' Now, the question is, who won?

— *Pennsylvania School Journal*, March 1887

•••

A COSMIC COINCIDENCE

Light travels 186,000 miles per second. The average diameter of Earth's orbit is 186 million miles.

So, on average, sunlight reaches us in a neat 500 seconds.

•••

STOP

The first arrest by telegraph took place in 1845. John Tawell poisoned his mistress at her home at Salt Hill and fled by train to

London, but police sent the following memorable message ahead to Paddington Station:

A MURDER HAD JUST BEEN COMMITTED AT SALT HILL AND THE SUSPECTED MURDERER WAS SEEN TO TAKE A FIRST CLASS TICKET TO LONDON BY THE TRAIN THAT LEFT SLOUGH AT 7.42 PM. HE IS IN THE GARB OF A KWAKER [the instrument lacked a Q] WITH A BROWN GREAT COAT ON WHICH REACHES HIS FEET. HE IS IN THE LAST COMPARTMENT OF THE SECOND FIRST-CLASS CARRIAGE.

In a London coffee tavern Tawell was confronted by a detective who asked, no doubt triumphantly, "Haven't you just come from Slough?" He was jailed, tried, convicted, and hanged.

• • •

THE MAIN COURSE

In 1913 Philadelphia housewife Margaret Nothe wrote her will in a book of kitchen recipes:

Chili Sauce Without Working

4 quarts of ripe tomatoes
4 small onions
4 green peppers
2 teacups of sugar
2 quarts of cider vinegar
2 ounces ground allspice
2 ounces cloves
2 ounces cinnamon
12 teaspoons salt

Chop tomatoes, onions and peppers fine, add the rest mixed together and bottle cold. Measure tomatoes when peeled. In case I die before my husband I leave everything to him.

Since it was recorded in Nothe's handwriting, a Pennsylvania probate court found it valid.

• • •

THE LOTTERY PARADOX

Imagine a lottery with 1,000 tickets.

It's rational to believe that one ticket will win.

But it's also rational to believe that the first ticket will not win—nor the second, nor the third, and so on.

And isn't that equivalent to believing that no ticket will win?

• • •

FOR THE RECORD

On Nov. 4, 1909, English pilot John Moore-Brabazon put a pig in a basket, tied it to a wing, and took off.

The basket read I AM THE FIRST PIG TO FLY.

• • •

THE APPLE CONUNDRUM

Two women are selling apples. The first sells 30 apples at 2 for $1, earning $15. The second sells 30 apples at 3 for $1, earning $10. So between them they've sold 60 apples for $25.

The next day they set the same goal but work together. They

sell 60 apples at 5 for $2, but they're puzzled to find that they've made only $24.

What became of the other dollar?

• • •

TIME-MACHINE JOURNALISM

Being the paper of record brings with it some odd responsibilities. On March 10, 1975, the *New York Times* inadvertently published the wrong dateline in its Late City editions, officially dating the day's news "March 10, 1075."

Modern readers would understand that this was a simple typo, of course, but the editors grew concerned that future historians might be confused to discover a *Times* issue from the Middle Ages. So the following day's issue contained a historic correction:

 In yesterday's issue, *The New York Times* did not report on riots in Milan and the subsequent murder of the lay religious reformer Erlembald. These events took place in 1075, the year given in the dateline under the nameplate on Page 1. The *Times* regrets both incidents.

PART TWO

HATS, HORSES, *and* HORATIO NELSON

HAT EXCHANGES

After leaving a Cambridge party, H.G. Wells realized he had picked up the wrong hat. The owner's name was inside the brim, but the hat fit well, and Wells liked it. So he sent a note instead:

"I stole your hat; I like your hat; I shall keep your hat. Whenever I look inside it I shall think of you and your excellent sherry and of the town of Cambridge. I take off your hat to you."

A letter from Mark Twain to William Dean Howells, London, July 3, 1899:

 Dear Howells,— . . .I've a lot of things to write you, but it's no use—I can't get time for anything these days. I must break off and write a postscript to Canon Wilberforce before I go to bed. This afternoon he left a luncheon-party half an hour ahead of the rest, and carried off my hat (which has *Mark Twain* in a big hand written in it). When the rest of us came out there was but one hat that would go on my head—it fitted exactly, too. So wore it away. It had no name in it, but the Canon was the only man who was absent. I wrote him a note at 8 p.m.; saying that for four hours I had not been able to take anything that did not belong to me, nor stretch a fact beyond the frontiers of truth, and my family were getting alarmed. Could he explain my trouble? And now at 8.30 p.m. comes a note from him to say that all the afternoon he has been exhibiting a wonder-compelling mental vivacity and grace of expression, etc., etc., and have I missed a hat? Our letters have crossed.

Yours ever,
Mark.

• • •

LITERARY REUNIONS

Browsing in a Paris bookshop in the 1920s, novelist Anne Parrish came upon an old copy of *Jack Frost and Other Stories*, a favorite from her childhood in Colorado. When she showed it to her husband, he found it was her own copy, inscribed with her name and address.

George Bernard Shaw once came across one of his own books in a used bookstore in London. He was surprised to find his own inscription inside—he had presented the book "with esteem" to a friend. He immediately bought the book and had it wrapped and delivered again, after adding a second inscription: "With renewed esteem, George Bernard Shaw."

• • •

THE NEW YORK ZOO HOAX

On Nov. 9, 1874, readers of the *New York Herald* were startled to learn of a mass escape from the Central Park Zoo—wild animals were roaming the streets as residents shot at them from tenement windows:

 There is no instance reported of any animals being hit, while it is believed many citizens were struck by the missiles. One policeman, Officer Lannigan of the Seventh Precinct, was wounded in the foot near Grand Street by a shot from a window during a chase after the striped hyena, which was mistaken by the crowd for a panther. This cowardly brute was finally killed by a bartender armed with a club.

The story reported 27 dead and 200 injured. It sparked a panic, as most readers overlooked the last paragraph, which stated that "the entire story given above is a pure fabrication." It had been intended to draw attention to inadequate safety precautions at the zoo.

The hoax's mastermind, Thomas B. Connery, had two consolations: His paper's circulation "did not drop by so much as one subscriber," he reported—and he'd got to watch the editor of the rival *New York Times* leave his home "with a brace of pistols, prepared to shoot the first animals that would cross his path."

• • •

THE CANDY BOMBER

In July 1948, 27-year-old Air Force lieutenant Gail Halvorsen was flying food and supplies into West Berlin, which was blockaded by the Soviet Union. One night he encountered a group of hungry children who had gathered near the runway to watch the planes land.

"They could speak a little English," he recalled later. "Their clothes were patched and they hadn't had gum and candy for two or three years. They barely had enough to eat."

Halvorsen gave them two sticks of gum and promised to drop more candy for them the next day from his C-54. He said he'd rock his wings so that they could distinguish him from the other planes. Then he returned to the base and spent the night tying bundles of candy to handkerchief parachutes.

Over the next three days he dropped candy to growing crowds of West German children. He had wanted to keep the project secret ("It seemed like something you weren't supposed to do"), but when a newsman snapped a photograph Halvorsen began receiving boxes of candy from all over the United States, many with parachutes already attached. Halvorsen went home in February 1949, and the blockade was lifted three months later.

In 1998, when Halvorsen returned to Berlin, a dignified 60-year-old man approached him. He said, "Fifty years ago I was a boy of 10 on my way to school. The clouds were very low with light rain. I could hear the planes landing, though I couldn't see them. Suddenly out of the mist came a parachute with a fresh Hershey chocolate bar from America. It landed right at my feet. I knew it was happening but couldn't believe it was for me. It took me a week to eat that candy bar. I hid it day and night. The chocolate was wonderful, but it wasn't the chocolate that was most important. What it meant was that someone in America knew I was here, in trouble and needed help. Someone in America cared. That parachute was something more important than candy. It represented hope. Hope that some day we would be free."

• • •

JURIST DICTION

Onomasticist Elsdon Coles Smith keeps a file on unfortunately named law firms. His list includes Ketcham & Cheatham in New York, Wind & Wind in Chicago, Ruff & Ready in Miami, and Dilly, Dally, Doolittle & Stahl in Akron.

Novelist Paul Auster insists he encountered an Irish firm

called Argue & Phibbs. ("This is a true story. If there are those who doubt me, I challenge them to visit Sligo and see for themselves if I have made it up or not.")

And Lyle Bland's lawyers, in Thomas Pynchon's *Gravity's Rainbow*, are Salitieri, Poore, Nash, DeBrutus & Short.

• • •

A NEW OUTLOOK

❝ A correspondent of the *Manchester Sporting Chronicle*, thinking that his horse was short-sighted, had his eyes examined by an oculist, who certified that the horse had a No. 7 eye and required concave glasses. These were obtained and fitted on to the horse's head. At first the horse was a little surprised, but rapidly showed signs of the keenest pleasure, and he now stands all the morning looking over the half-door of his stable with his spectacles on, gazing around him with an air of sedate enjoyment. When driven his manner is altogether changed from his former timidity; but if pastured without his spectacles on, he hangs about the gate whinnying in a plaintive minor key. If the spectacles are replaced he kicks up his heels and scampers up and down the pasture with delight.

— *British Veterinary Journal*, March 1888

• • •

IN A WORD

exsibilation

n. the act of hissing someone off the stage

vespertilionize
v. to turn into a bat

jussulent
adj. full of broth or soup

illeist
n. one who refers to himself in the third person

• • •

EXPRESS

On June 12, 1940, a man strolled onto the platform at Ireland's Dingle light railway station and asked some workers when the next train would depart for Tralee.

The men stared at him, and one said, "The last train for Tralee left here 14 years ago. I reckon it might be another 14 years before the next train will leave."

Two hours later the man, Walter Simon, was in a local jail cell. It turned out he was a German spy who had landed that evening by U-boat at Dingle Bay. His spying career was over.

• • •

A HIGHER STAR

At a dinner, Oliver Herford found himself sitting next to a very serious young woman.

"Tell me, Mr. Herford," she said. "Have you no ambition beyond making people laugh?"

"Yes, I have," he replied. "And someday I hope to gratify it."

"Please tell me," she said eagerly. "What is it?"

He said, "I want to throw an egg into an electric fan."

• • •

SPECIAL DELIVERY

This is the Flammarion woodcut, so named because it first appeared in Camille Flammarion's 1888 book *L'Atmosphère*. No one knows who created it; it's thought to depict a medieval pilgrim who discovers the point where earth and sky meet.

Flammarion's book itself seemed touched by magic. As the astronomer was completing a chapter on the force of the wind, a sudden gale blew the last few pages out the window and off in a whirlwind among the trees. Then a downpour started, and Flammarion gave them up as lost.

He was astonished, then, a few days later when his printer delivered the full chapter, with no pages missing.

It seems the porter who normally brought Flammarion's proof sheets had been returning to his office when he noticed the sodden manuscript leaves on the ground. He assumed that he himself had dropped them and so had collected them and carried them to the printer without telling anyone.

"Remember," Flammarion writes, "it was a chapter on the strange doings of the wind."

· · ·

CHAPTER AND VERSE

As he was visiting his parishioners one Saturday afternoon, a new pastor stopped at one house and found that no one answered the door. It was clear that someone was home, but he knocked repeatedly and nobody appeared. Finally he pulled out his card, wrote "Revelation 3:20" on the back, and left it in the door.

That Sunday he found the card in the collection basket. Below his message someone had written "Genesis 3:10."

Revelation 3:20 reads, "Behold I stand at the door, and knock: if any man hear my voice, and open the door, I will come in to him, and will dine with him, and he with me."

Genesis 3:10 reads, "And he said, I heard thy voice in the garden, and I was afraid, because I was naked."

· · ·

HORSE SENSE

John Raymond Godley (1920-2006), Lord Kilbracken, was a respected writer and journalist, but he's remembered mostly for a peculiar talent: He dreamed the winners of horse races.

- While an undergraduate at Oxford in 1946, he dreamed he was reading racing results in a newspaper. Two of the winners were Bindal and Juladin, horses he knew from his waking life. In the morning he discovered that both would be running that afternoon. He bet on both, and both won.

- A month later, vacationing in Ireland, he awoke with the name Tubermore in his mind. He called the local postmistress the following day, and she told him that a Tuberose was running that day. He won, at odds of 100 to 6.
- In July he dreamed that a bookie's clerk told him a horse named Monumentor had won a race. He found in the morning that a Mentores would be running that day. He bet and won.
- In June 1947 he dreamed he was watching one race in which he recognized jockey Edgar Britt, then watched a second race won by a horse called The Bogie. He woke to find that Britt was riding that day, and that a horse called The Brogue would be running in the race that followed. This time he sealed his picks in a time-stamped envelope in the presence of witnesses. Both horses won.
- In 1949 he dreamed he read the name Timocrat in the *Mirror*'s racing sheet. He discovered that Timocrat was running the next day; he bet and won.

And so on. He couldn't summon the dreams, of course, and the horses he picked didn't invariably win. But even nine years later a dream led him to the winner of the Grand National. "I can offer no explanation, rational or irrational," he wrote in a memoir. "Make your own deductions, but accept my facts as true."

• • •

UNQUOTE

"A sadist is a person who is kind to a masochist."

—Arthur Koestler

• • •

SPENT TEARS

George Moore was writing in his study when his aunt entered.

"I have sad news for you, Mr. Moore," she said. "I regret to inform you that your friend Martin Ross is dead."

Moore lowered his pen, sighed, and gazed quietly around him at the trappings of his long literary life. "How sad," he said, "how sad. Here I am in the midst of this, alive . . .and my friend, my dear friend, Edmund Gosse, dead."

"I beg your pardon, Mr. Moore," the lady put in gently. "It is Martin Ross who is dead, not Edmund Gosse."

Moore said, "Surely you don't expect me to go through all that again?"

• • •

UNDEFINED

The U.S. dime does not state its value. It's labeled simply "one dime."

• • •

C STORY

You arrive in purgatory to find it's just a typewriter on a desk. As you take your seat, you notice that the C key is glowing faintly.

A demon says, "All you have to do is type the natural numbers, in order: ONE, TWO, and so on. The first time you strike the C key, you'll be released into paradise."

That doesn't sound too bad. Assuming it takes 10 seconds on average to type each number (and that you spell each correctly, in English), how much time will pass before you first type the letter C?

(See Answers and Solutions)

• • •

MANAGERESE

Henry Ford told a visitor to the Ford Motor Company that there were exactly 4,719 parts in a finished car.

Impressed, the visitor asked the supervising engineer if this were true.

"I'm sure I don't know," said the engineer. "I can't think of a more useless piece of information."

• • •

TESTAMENT

Dorothy Parker named her pet canary Onan, "because he spills his seed upon the ground."

• • •

OWNEY

If there's a trophy for the world's best-traveled canine, it belongs to Owney, a mixed-breed terrier who wandered into the Albany post office in 1888. The workers found he was attracted to mail bags, following them onto wagons and eventually trains, so they adopted him as a mascot.

They gave him a collar ("Owney, Post Office, Albany, New York") and sent him off through the system, where he became a sort of perpetual parcel. Each time he returned to Albany he bore a new assortment of tokens and tags from mail clerks around the country; eventually these numbered 1,017. In 1895 he traveled entirely around the world via train and steamship.

He retired in 1897 due to old age, and his carefully preserved remains are on display in the U.S. Postal Museum in Washington, D.C.

• • •

A POOR SHOWING

Charlie Chaplin once lost a Charlie Chaplin lookalike contest. He didn't even make the finals.

Afterward he told a reporter that he was "tempted to give lessons in the Chaplin walk, out of pity as well as in the desire to see the thing done correctly."

• • •

SCRABBLE HEAVEN

The most frequently used letters of the English alphabet, in order, are ETAOIN SHRDLU.

They can be rearranged to spell SOUTH IRELAND.

• • •

UNQUOTE

"Madam, it is the hardest thing in the world to be in love, and yet attend to business. A gentleman asked me this morning, 'What news from Lisbon?' and I answered, 'She is exquisitely handsome.'"

—Richard Steele

• • •

ALCOHOL PROBLEM

Fill one glass with wine and another with water. Transfer a teaspoonful of wine from the first glass into the second. Then transfer a teaspoonful of that mixture back into the first glass. Now, is there more wine in the water or water in the wine?

Most people will predict it's the former, but in fact the two quantities will always be the same. Can you see why?

• • •

RUN TOPPERS

Let's play a game. We'll each name three consecutive outcomes of a coin toss (for example, tails-heads-heads, or THH). Then we'll flip a coin repeatedly until one of our chosen runs appears. That player wins.

Is there any strategy you can take to improve your chance of beating me? Strangely, there is. When I've named my triplet (say, HTH), take the complement of the center symbol and add it to the beginning, and then discard the last symbol (here yielding HHT). This new triplet will be more likely to appear than mine.

The remarkable thing is that *this always works*. No matter what triplet I pick, this method will always produce a triplet that is more likely to appear than mine. It was discovered by Barry Wolk of the University of Manitoba, building on a discovery by Walter Penney.

• • •

BUSY

On May 29, 1933, *Harper's Bazaar* editor Art Samuels was awaiting a piece by the notoriously unreliable Robert Benchley when he received six successive telegrams:

> AM TAKING CARE OF MY SICK MOTHER.
> AM ACTING AS GUIDE FOR HUNTING PARTY.
> AM INSPECTING NEW PACKARD ENGINES.
> AM JUDGING ORANGE BLOSSOM CARNIVAL.
> AM BEING INDUCTED INTO INDIAN TRIBE.
> AM WORKING ON PICTURE WITH GRETA GARBO.

All bore the current date, but their origins were listed as Worcester, Massachusetts; Presque Isle, Maine; Detroit, Michigan; Miami Beach, Florida; Santa Fe, New Mexico; and Hollywood, California. Samuels wrote back GATHER YOU HAVEN'T DONE THE PIECE.

Benchley avoided another engagement by having his mother send this wire from Massachusetts:

> SORRY I CAN'T ATTEND LUNCHEON TODAY BECAUSE I AM IN BOSTON. DON'T KNOW WHY I AM IN BOSTON BUT IT MUST BE IMPORTANT BECAUSE HERE I AM.
> BENCHLEY

• • •

THE WOODEN HORSE

In 1943, authorities at a German POW camp in Poland discovered that three prisoners were missing. A considerable space separated the prisoners' huts from the perimeter fence, so at first it wasn't clear how they'd escaped.

But the three inmates had something in common—all three had exercised during the day on a vaulting horse in the yard. On investigating, the Germans discovered a 100-foot tunnel leading from that spot to an opening beyond the fence.

The truth became clear. Each day, the prisoners had carried the horse to the same spot with a man hidden inside. While they exercised, the hidden man had used a bowl to lengthen the tunnel, then hid again in the horse as it was carried back inside. The Germans had used siesmographs to detect tunneling, but the prisoners' vaulting had masked the sounds of their digging.

All three escapees—Eric Williams, Michael Codner, and Oliver Philpot—reached neutral Sweden and were reunited with their families.

• • •

TURNABOUT

Two business partners asked their lawyer to hold $20,000, making him promise to get both of their signatures before disbursing any of it.

As soon as one partner left town, the other pressed the lawyer for $15,000, citing an emergency. The lawyer reluctantly gave it to him, and he disappeared.

On his return, the other partner was irate, so the lawyer explained that he had donated the $15,000 out of his own pocket.

"Then give me the $20,000 you're holding," said the partner.

"All right," said the lawyer. "Give me the two signatures."

• • •

"WHO CAN TELL?"

From Don Lemon, *Everybody's Illustrated Book of Puzzles*, 1890:

 Twice six are eight of us,
Six are but three of us,
Nine are but four of us,
What can we possibly be?

Would you know more of us?
I'll tell you more of us.
Twelve are but six of us,
Five are but four of us, now do you see?

(See Answers and Solutions)

• • •

SPECIAL DELIVERY

Where there's a will, there's a way. In 1849, Henry Box Brown escaped slavery by mailing himself to Philadelphia.

Brown stood 5'8" and weighed 200 pounds, and he spent 26 hours in a box measuring 2'8" x 2' x 3'. Unfortunately, he spent a lot of it upside down. "I felt my eyes swelling as if they would burst from their sockets," he later wrote, "and the veins on my temples were dreadfully distended with pressure of blood upon my head." The trip from Richmond covered 275 miles by overland express stage wagon.

When the box was opened, his first words were "How do you do, gentlemen?"

• • •

A GENEROUS COMMISSION

Shortly before Nelson left England for the last time, he found himself sitting next to Benjamin West at an honorary dinner. The admiral complimented the painter on his *Death of Wolfe* and asked why he had produced no more pictures like it.

"Because, my lord," West said, "there are no more subjects." He said he feared that Nelson's dauntless courage might produce another such scene, and "if it should, I shall certainly avail myself of it."

"Will you, Mr. West?" Nelson said. "Then I hope I shall die in the next battle."

He got his wish—West found himself painting *The Death of Nelson* the following year.

• • •

• • •

PRECOCIOUS

Thomas Macaulay was a child prodigy—and, one imagines, a trial to his parents:

- On seeing a chimney as a toddler, he asked his father, "Is that hell?"
- At 3 his mother told him he must learn to study without his bread and butter. He said, "Yes, mama, industry shall be my bread and attention my butter."
- When he was 4 years old a servant spilled hot coffee on his legs; when the hostess inquired how he was feeling, he said, "Thank you, madam, the agony is abated."
- When a housemaid threw away some oyster shells he'd been using to fence a garden plot, he marched into the drawing room and said, "Cursed be Sally, for it is written, 'Cursed be he that removeth his neighbor's landmark.'"

Reputedly his great gifts stayed with him throughout his life: As an old man he recited two poems he hadn't seen since age 13.

• • •

UNQUOTE

"It is annoying to be honest to no purpose."

—Ovid

• • •

NOTED

In November 1941 a U-boat torpedoed the British battleship *Barham*, but the Germans didn't realize they'd hit it. The British Admiralty managed to keep the loss a secret for two months, but in the interval a Scottish spiritualist named Helen Duncan announced that the *Barham* had sunk. She said she'd heard the news from a dead sailor.

The British authorities arrested Duncan, hoping to discredit her story. They appealed to an old law against fraudulent "spiritual" activity . . .which unfortunately was called the British Witchcraft Act of 1735.

So: History records that a practicing medium who revealed an "unknowable" secret at a séance in 1941 was convicted under a witchcraft law. She served 9 months.

• • •

THE LOCK KEY

Two adjoining lakes are connected by a lock. The lakes differ by 2 meters in elevation. To move from the lower lake to the upper, a boat enters the lock, the gate is closed behind it, water is added to the lock chamber until its level matches that of the upper lake, and then the boat passes out through the upper gate.

Now suppose two boats do this in succession. The first boat weighs 50 tons, the second only 5 tons. How much more water must be used to raise the small boat than the large one?

(See Answers and Solutions)

• • •

CONSULTATION

A letter from Lewis Carroll to 14-year-old Wilton Rix:

 Honoured Sir,

Understanding you to be a distinguished algebraist (i.e. distinguished from other algebraists by different face, different height, etc.), I beg to submit to you a difficulty which distresses me much.

If x and y are each equal to '1,' it is plain that

$2 \times (x^2 - y^2) = 0$, and also that $5 \times (x - y) = 0$.

Hence $2 \times (x^2 - y^2) = 5 \times (x - y)$.

Now divide each side of this equation by $(x - y)$.

Then $2 \times (x + y) = 5$.

But $(x + y) = (1 + 1)$, i.e. $= 2$.

So that $2 \times 2 = 5$.

Ever since this painful fact has been forced upon me, I have not slept more than 8 hours a night, and have not been able to eat more than 3 meals a day.

I trust you will pity me and will kindly explain the difficulty to

Your obliged, Lewis Carroll

• • •

BAD ADVICE

In 1887, president Grover Cleveland welcomed an old friend to the White House. Weary of the office, he said to the man's 5-year-old son, "My little man, I am making a strange wish for you. It is that you may never be president of the United States."

The boy was Franklin Roosevelt.

• • •

AS ABOVE, SO BELOW

NINETY-SEVEN is the longest number name with strictly alternating vowels and consonants. . .

. . .unless you count NEGATIVE NINETY-SEVEN.

• • •

THE LAST WAVE

On the night of Dec. 12, 1978, the German barge carrier *München* issued a distress call in the North Atlantic. A week's search collected four empty life rafts, but the ship itself was never found.

Two months later another ship discovered the *München*'s starboard lifeboat. Its supporting pins had been bent, suggesting that a huge force had passed along the *München* from fore to aft, tearing the boat from its supports.

That boat had hung 20 meters above the waterline. What did the *München* encounter that night?

• • •

PALACE LIFE

   When [Edward IV's jester John] Scogin was banished out of France, he filled his shooes full of French earth, and came into England, and went into the king's court, and as soone as he came to the court, the king said to him: I did charge thee that thou shouldest never tread upon my ground of England. It is true, said Scogin, and no more I doe. What! traytor, said the king, whose ground is that thou standest on now? Scogin said: I stand upon the French king's ground, and that you shall see; and first he put off the one shooe, and it was full of earth. Then said Scogin: this earth I brought out of France. Then said the king: I charge thee never to looke me more in the face.

— *Scoggin's Jests*, 1626

PART THREE

JESSE JAMES, PENNIES
and THE NORTH POLE

THE POPGUN WAR

Brothers Alphonse, Kenneth, and Mayo Prud'homme were playing with a foot-long toy cannon in Natchitoches, La., in September 1941 when they saw a man peering at them through binoculars from the opposite side of the Cane River. "We just fired a shot at him to see what would happen," Kenneth remembered later. "He bailed out of the tree and went flying back down the road in a cloud of dust."

Presently the man returned with infantry. "They started shooting back at us, and when they'd shoot, we'd shoot back."

This went on for half an hour, escalating gradually. The boys' father added firecrackers to their arsenal; their opponents set up smoke screens and readied a .155 howitzer. At last an Army officer appeared at their side and said, "Mr. Prud'homme, do you mind calling off your boys? You're holding up our war."

The boys, ages 14, 12, and 9, had interrupted war games involving 400,000 troops spread over 3,400 square miles in preparation for America's entry into World War II. At the sound of the cannon, George S. Patton had stopped his Blue convoy and engaged what he thought was the opposing Red army. His men were firing blanks, but the maneuvers were real.

"That's my one claim to fame," Kenneth told an Army magazine writer in 2009. "I defeated General Patton."

• • •

DICTION AIRY

In 1856 Samuel Hoshour reflected that students might learn new words more easily if they were presented in context rather than in long gray lists of definitions. The result was *Letters to Squire Pedant*, an imaginary correspondence salted with ten-dollar vocabulary words:

 Dear Sir, At my decession from you; your final alloquy, and concinnous deport laid me under a reasonable obstriction to impart to you, a pantography of the occidental domain upon which I had placed my ophthalmic organs. I now merge my plumous implement of chirography into the atramental fluid, to exonerate myself of that obstriction. From my earliest juvenility, I possessed an indomitable proclivity to lead those that are given to the lection of my lucubrations, to the *inception* of occurrences. And it would be a dilucid evagation from my accustomary route, would I not now insist upon a regression of your mind to the locality where we imparted mutual valedictions.

Unfortunately, he gets a bit carried away. "Longevous Sir," begins Letter IV, "The day sequacious to the vesper on which I effectuated in a certain cabaret an exsiccation of my habiliments by torrefaction, was not very inservient to the progress of a pedestrious emigrant."

• • •

A HIKING PUZZLE

Suppose a man sets out to climb a mountain at sunrise, arriving at the top at sunset. He sleeps at the top and descends the following day, traveling somewhat more quickly downhill. Prove that there's a point on the path that he will pass at the same time on both days.

(See Answers and Solutions)

• • •

ROUNDABOUT

SENSUOUSNESSES is a circular palindrome—when it is written in a circle, the same word can be descried whether the letters are read clockwise or counter-clockwise.

• • •

RIMSHOT

Two atoms are walking down the street.
One says, "Wait, I think I lost an electron."
The other says, "Are you sure?"
The first one says, "Yes, I'm positive."

• • •

SUCCINCT

Pun fans claim that Sir Francis Drake reported the defeat of the Spanish Armada with a single word: "Cantharides" (an aphrodisiac; hence "The Spanish fly").

When Sir Charles Napier took the Indian province of Sindh in 1843, he supposedly sent a one-word report to the British war office: *Peccavi* (Latin for "I have sinned").

When Lord Dalhousie annexed Oudh in the 1850s, he's said to have sent a dispatch of a single word: *Vovi* (I vowed, or "I've Oudh").

And when Lord Clyde captured Lucknow in 1857, he supposedly responded, *"Nunc fortunatus sum"* ("I am in luck now").

A dinner guest once bet her friends that she could get Calvin Coolidge to say at least three words during the meal. He told her, "You lose."

• • •

TRIPLE PLAY

Jesse James once sought shelter at a lonely farmhouse. The widow there apologized for her poor hospitality. She said she had very little money and despaired of paying the debt collector, who was coming imminently to demand $1,400.

James gave her $1,400 and told her to get a receipt. Then he hid outside and watched the road.

The debt collector arrived, looking grim, and entered the house. A few minutes later he emerged, looking pleased.

James accosted him, took back the $1,400, and rode off.

• • •

SELF-EXPRESSION

The first few powers of 5 share a curious property—their digits can be rearranged to express their value:

$$25 = 5^2$$
$$125 = 5^{1 + 2}$$
$$625 = 5^{6 - 2}$$
$$3125 = (3 + (1 \times 2))^5$$
$$15625 = 5^6 \times 1^{25}$$
$$78125 = 5^7 \times 1^{82}$$

It's conjectured that all powers of 5 have this property. But no one's proved it yet.

• • •

A PROFESSIONAL STUDENT

According to his transcript, George P. Burdell has been a student at Georgia Tech since 1927. How? He was invented out of thin air when student Ed Smith received two enrollment forms. With Smith's help, "Burdell" attended all his friend's classes and took all the same exams.

For a nonexistent person, Burdell turned out to be pretty ambitious. Smith graduated in 1930, but his invisible friend stuck around, adopted by other students. He eventually earned a master's degree and became an official alumnus, then flew 12 bombing missions over Europe in World War II. In 1969 he signed up for a whopping 3,000 credit hours at Georgia Tech—and began a 12-year term on *MAD* magazine's board of directors. In 2001 he was briefly the leading contender among voters for *TIME* magazine's person of the year.

Strangely, after 79 years of school Burdell is still only a sophomore. He's majoring in civil engineering, according to a recent report card.

• • •

STRANGE WEATHER

" An optical illusion or mirage was seen by three or four farmers a few miles from this city a few days since, the appearance of which no one is able philosophically to account for. The facts are these: A gentleman, while plowing in a field with several others, about 7 P.M., happened to glance toward the sky, which was cloudless, and saw apparently, about half a mile off in a westerly direction, an opaque substance, resembling a white horse, with head, neck, limbs, and tail clearly defined, swimming in the clear atmosphere. It appeared to be moving its limbs as if engaged in swimming, moving its head from side to side, always ascending at an angle of about 45°. He rubbed his eyes to convince himself that he was not dreaming, and looked again; but there it still was, still apparently swimming and ascending in ether. He called to the men, about 100 yards off, and told them to look up, and tell him what they saw. They declared they saw a white horse swimming in the sky, and were badly frightened. Our informant, neither superstitious nor nervous, sat down and watched the phantasm, (if we may so call it,) until is disappeared in space, always going in the same direction, and moving in the same manner. No one can account for the mirage, or illusion, except upon the uneven state of the atmosphere. Illusions of a different appearance have been seen at different times, in the same vicinity, frightening the superstitious and laughed at by the skeptical.

— Telegram from Parkersburg, W.Va., to the *Cincinnati Commercial*, reprinted in the *New York Times*, July 8, 1878

• • •

CIVIC-MINDED

COMMUNICATORIALLY contains COMMUNITY, COUNTRY, COUNTY, and CITY, each in the proper order.

• • •

THE CLAIRVOYANT PENNY

Mathematician Thomas Storer offers a foolproof way to foretell the future: Flip a penny and ask it a yes-or-no question. Heads means yes, tails means no.

How can you be sure the answer is accurate? Simple: Flip it again and ask, "Will your present answer have the same truth value as your previous answer?"

- Suppose the answer is yes. This is either true or false. If it's true, then the original response was true. If it's false, then the truth value of the original response is not false, i.e., it's true.

- If the answer to the second question is no, this too is either true or false. If it's true, then the original response was true. If it's false, then the original response was not false, i.e., true.

Since all the outcomes agree, the penny's original response is guaranteed to be correct.

• • •

OH

Croesus asked the oracle at Delphi whether he should attack the Persians. She replied that if he went to war, he would destroy a great empire.

Croesus attacked, but the Persians beat him back, invaded his kingdom, and threw him into chains. He sent another message to the oracle: "Why did you deceive me?"

She replied that she had not deceived him—he had indeed destroyed a great empire.

• • •

HARE REMOVER

Paul Armand-Delille was angry at the damage that rabbits were doing to his French estate, so on June 14, 1952, he inoculated two of them with a virus, *Myxomatosis cuniculi*, that he knew had curbed rabbit populations in Australia.

It, um, worked. Within 6 weeks, 98 percent of his rabbits were dead—and by the end of 1954, so were 90 percent of the rabbits in France.

Armand-Delille was charged one franc for illegally spreading an animal disease, then given a medal for services to agriculture.

The medal depicts Armand-Delille on one side and a dead rabbit on the other.

• • •

CRASHPROOF

In 1895, Henry Latimer Simmons invented ramp-shaped railroad cars:

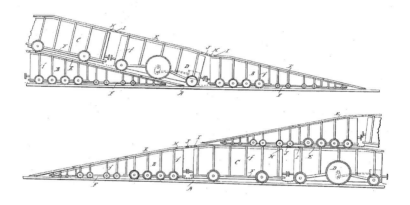

"When one train meets or overtakes another train, one train will run up the rails carried by the other train, and will run along the rails and descend onto the rails at the other end of the lower train."

With good design, everybody wins.

• • •

THE PENNY GAME

Two robots are playing a game. Between them is a pile of coins. Each robot, on its turn, can take either one or two coins from the pile. So long as each elects to take one coin, play continues until the pile is exhausted. If either elects to take two, the remaining coins vanish and the game ends.

One might think that the best plan would be always to take a single coin, but if both players are rational and know it, the first player will immediately take two pennies and end the game.

He reasons thus: If there were only two pennies in the pile, I'd benefit most by taking both of them rather than just one. Now suppose there were three pennies. If I took only one, then I would leave my opponent in the position I just imagined, and being rational he'd take both remaining pennies. Therefore I should take two of the three.

And so on backward, up to any arbitrary number of pennies. Paradoxically, it seems, improvident greed is more rational than constructive cooperation.

• • •

OH, NEVER MIND

" Zhuangzi and Huizi were strolling along the dam of the Hao Waterfall when Zhuangzi said, 'See how the minnows come out and dart around where they please! That's what fish really enjoy!'

Huizi said, 'You're not a fish—how do you know what fish enjoy?'

Zhuangzi said, 'You're not I, so how do you know I don't know what fish enjoy?'

Huizi said, 'I'm not you, so I certainly don't know what you know. On the other hand, you're certainly not a fish—so that still proves you don't know what fish enjoy!'

Zhuangzi said, 'Let's go back to your original question,

please. You asked me how I know what fish enjoy—so you already knew I knew it when you asked the question. I know it by standing here beside the Hao.'

— Zhuangzi, China, fourth century B.C.

• • •

POP FLY

In August 1960, the submarine U.S.S. *Seadragon* surfaced at the North Pole. During their visit, the crew laid out a softball diamond with the pitcher's mound at the pole.

"If you hit a home run you circumnavigated the globe," recalled crew member Alfred S. McLaren. "If you hit the ball into right field, it was across the international date line into tomorrow, and if the right fielder caught it, he threw it back into yesterday."

Captain George P. Steele later claimed he hit a fly ball at 4 p.m. Wednesday that wasn't caught until 4 a.m. Thursday.

• • •

HMM

The most common birthday in the United States is Oct. 5.

That's 274 days after New Year's Eve—the length of the average pregnancy.

• • •

CAT AS COAUTHOR

Physicist J.H. Hetherington had already typed up a physics paper in 1975 when he learned of an unfortunate style rule: *Physical*

Review Letters does not accept the pronoun *we* in single-author papers.

Hetherington didn't want to retype the paper—this was before word processors had become widespread—so he added his cat as a second author ("F.D.C. Willard," for "*Felis Domesticus* Chester Willard.")

"Why was I willing to do such an irreverent thing? Against it was the fact that most of us are paid partly by how many papers we publish, and there is some dilution of the effect of the paper on one's reputation when it is shared by another author. On the other hand, I did not ignore completely the publicity value, either. If it eventually proved to be correct, people would remember the paper more if the anomalous authorship were known. In any case I went ahead and did it and have generally not been sorry. Most people are amused by the concept, only editors, for some reason, seem to find little humour in the story."

Chester is believed to be the only cat who has published research in low-temperature physics. "When reprints arrived, I inked F.D.C. Willard's paw and he and I signed about 10 reprints which I sent to a few friends," Hetherington later recalled. "The story has now been told many times and my wife can add that she sleeps with both authors!"

• • •

ILL-STARRED

For stewardess Violet Jessop, bad luck came in threes. In 1911 she was working on the RMS *Olympic* when it collided with a British warship off the Isle of Wight.

A few months later she took a position on the *Titanic*, which sank in the North Atlantic in 1912. Her lifeboat was picked up by the *Carpathia*.

And in 1916 she was working as a nurse on the hospital ship *Britannic* when it struck a mine in the Aegean Sea and went down.

By this time she was philosophical. Though the *Britannic* sank in less than 50 minutes, she took care to rescue her toothbrush, "because there had always been much fun at my expense after the *Titanic*, when I complained of my inability to get a toothbrush on the *Carpathia*. I recalled [my brother's] joking advice: 'Never undertake another disaster without first making sure of your toothbrush.'"

After that her bad luck ceased. She lived without incident for another 55 years and died of heart failure in 1971.

• • •

A REMADE MAN

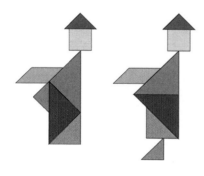

A tangram paradox by Sam Loyd. Each of these gentlemen is assembled from the same seven pieces. Yet one has a foot and the other doesn't. How is this possible?

• • •

A PENNY SAVED

 Recipe to keep a person warm the whole winter with a single Billet of Wood.—Take a billet of wood the ordinary size, run up into the garret with it as quick as you can, throw it out of the garret window; run down after it (not out of the garret window mind) as fast as possible; repeat this till you are warm, and as often as occasion may require. It will never fail to have the desired effect whilst you are able to use it.—Probatum est.

— *Oracle and Public Advertiser*, Nov. 24, 1796

• • •

ROMANCE AT SHORT NOTICE

Bata Kindai Amgoza ibn LoBagola told an inspiring story: Born in West Africa, he wandered to the sea at age 7 and found himself aboard a steamer bound for Scotland. From there he made his way to the United States, where he took up lecturing. His 1930 autobiography, *LoBagola; An African Savage's Own Story*, gives vivid details about life in the bush:

> If you should climb a tree, the lion can easily get help from the elephant, because the elephant and the lion are friendly. . . .[T]he lion tells the elephant that it wants you down from the tree, and the elephant shakes the tree or pulls it up by the roots, and down you come.

The truth was more prosaic: His real name was Joseph Lee and he was born in Baltimore. "Small opportunities," wrote Demosthenes, "are often the beginning of great enterprises."

• • •

HOW TO WIN SIX MILLION DOLLARS

Summon six millionaires and invite them to stake their fortunes on a single hand of poker. They will eagerly agree. Open a new deck of cards, discard the jokers, and ask the millionaires to cut (but not shuffle!) the deck as many times as they like. Then deal seven hands, ostentatiously dealing your own second and fourth cards from the bottom of the deck.

The millionaires may be reluctant to object to this, as all six of them will be holding full houses. (This works—try it.) But "See here," they will finally say. "What was that business with the bottom-dealing? You're up to something. We insist that you discard that hand." Look hurt, then deal yourself a new hand.

You'll likely be holding a straight flush.

• • •

E PLURIBUS UNUM

11111111111111111111111111111111111111111111111111111111111111111
11111111111111111111111111111111111111111111111111111111111111111
11111111111111111111111111111111111111111111111111111111111111111
11111111111111111111111111111111111111111111111111111111111111111
11111111111111111111111111111111111111111111111111111111111111111
11111111111111111111111111111111111111111111111111111111111111111
11111111111111111111111111111111111111111111111111111111111111111
11111111111111111111111111111111111111111111111111111111111111111
11111111111111111111111111111111111111111111111111111111111111111
11111111111111111111111111111111111111111111111111111111111111111
11111111111111111111111111111111111111111111111111111111111111111
11111111111111111111111111111111111111111111111111111111111111111
11111111111111111111111111111111111111111111111111111111111111111
11111111111111111111111111111111111111111111111111111111111111111
11111111111111111111111111111111111111111111111111111111111111111
1111111111111111111111111111111111111 is prime.

•••

UNQUOTE

"Where the press is free,
and every man able to read,
all is safe."
—Thomas Jefferson

•••

DISCOUNT TRAVEL

When 5-year-old May Pierstorff asked to visit her grandmother, her parents had no money to buy a rail ticket.

So they mailed her.

On Feb. 19, 1914, May's parents presented her at the post office in Grangeville, Idaho, and proposed mailing her parcel post to Lewiston, some 75 miles away. The postmaster found that the "package" was just under the 50-pound weight limit, so he winked at their plan, classed May as a baby chick, and attached 53 cents in stamps to her coat. May passed the entire trip in the train's mail compartment—and was duly delivered to her grandparents in Lewiston by mail clerk Leonard Mochel.

•••

WITCHCRAFT

In 1643, Marin Mersenne wrote to Pierre de Fermat asking whether 100895598169 were a prime number.

Fermat replied immediately that it's the product of 898423 and 112303, both of which are prime.

To this day, no one knows how he knew this. Has a powerful factoring technique been lost?

• • •

THE JUDGE'S CONUNDRUM

In the desert, a bandit shoots a sheriff. The wounded sheriff rides into town, where the outraged townspeople form a mob. They track the bandit to his desert hideout and hang him. The sheriff dies a few days later.

Now: Did the bandit kill the sheriff? If so . . .when and where?

• • •

IN A WORD

andabatarian
adj. struggling while blindfolded

shunpike
n. a side road taken to avoid turnpike tolls or traffic

coenaculous
adj. loving supper

mulomedic
adj. relating to the medical care of mules

• • •

HEADS OF STATE

Ten senators are about to enter Congress when a barrage of snowballs knocks off their tophats. Each retrieves a hat at random. What is the probability that exactly nine of them receive their own hats?

(See Answers and Solutions)

• • •

THE HANDICAPPER

In the 1740s, workers at a stable near Cambridge noticed that a cat had taken a peculiar fancy to one of the horses there. She was always near him, they found, sitting on his back or nestling nearby in the manger.

Her attachment proved so great that when the stallion died in 1754 "she sat upon him after he was dead in the building erected for him, and followed him to the place where he was buried under a gateway near the running stable; sat upon him there till he was buried, then went away, and never was seen again, till found dead in the hayloft"—apparently of grief.

The cat's name is not recorded, but she certainly could pick horses: The stallion was the Godolphin Arabian, now revered as the founder of modern thoroughbred racing stock. His direct descendants include both Seabiscuit and Man o' War.

• • •

SACK RACE

After losing a bet in April 1864, shopkeeper Reuel Gridley carried a 50-pound sack of flour through the little town of Austin,

Nev. In a saloon afterward, someone proposed selling the flour at auction for the benefit of wounded Union soldiers. The suggestion was adopted on the spot, and the winning bid, $250, came from a local mill worker.

When Gridley asked where to deliver the sack, the man said, "Nowhere—sell it again."

Thus was born a unique enterprise: Three hundred people paid a total of $8,000 for the same sack of flour that day, and soon Gridley went on tour through other Nevada mining towns, raising tens of thousands of dollars by selling it repeatedly. By the war's end he had extended the tour through California, New York, and St. Louis and raised $150,000, a fortune for the time. Mark Twain wrote, "This is probably the only instance on record where common family flour brought three thousand dollars a pound in the public market."

• • •

RECURSIVE GRATITUDE

Mathematician J.E. Littlewood once wrote a paper for the French journal *Comptes Rendus*. A Prof. M. Riesz did the translation, and at the end Littlewood found three footnotes:

 I am greatly indebted to Prof. Riesz for translating the present paper.

> I am indebted to Prof. Riesz for translating the preceding footnote.

> I am indebted to Prof. Riesz for translating the preceding footnote.

Littlewood notes that this could have gone on indefinitely but "I stop legitimately at number 3: however little French I know I am capable of copying a French sentence."

• • •

UNQUOTE

"After I'm dead I'd rather have people ask why I have no
monument than why I have one."

—Cato the Elder

• • •

SITZFLEISCH

In the days before chess clocks, a player might wait for hours
while his opponent decided on a move.

Paul Morphy's companion Frederick Milnes Edge remarked
that "[József] Szén was so frightfully slow, even in ordinary
games, that he would have worn out 200 francs' worth of his opponent's pantaloons before the match was half through."

The most notorious slowpoke in England was Elijah "The
Bristol Sloth" Williams: In the fourth game of his London match
against Henry Thomas Buckle in 1851, Williams lavished such
exquisite care on his 25th move that Buckle had time to write
two chapters of his *History of Civilization.*

Buckle won. "The slowness of genius is hard to bear," he said,
"but the slowness of mediocrity is intolerable."

• • •

UNWELCOME COINCIDENCE

Abraham Lincoln's son Robert seemed to carry an odd curse—
he was present or nearby at three successive presidential assassinations:

- On April 14, 1865, his parents invited him to accompany them to Ford's Theater. He remained at the White House and heard of his father's death near midnight.
- On July 2, 1881, he was an eyewitness to Garfield's assassination at Washington's Sixth Street Train Station.
- On Sept. 6, 1901, he was present at the Pan-American Exposition in Buffalo, N.Y., when McKinley was shot.

In 1863, a stranger saved his life in a Jersey City train station. The stranger was Edwin Booth—the brother of John Wilkes Booth, his father's future assassin.

• • •

ON-THE-JOB TRAINING

In the 1960s, biologist Karen Pryor was training two female rough-toothed dolphins to perform in a show at Hawaii's Sea Life Park. Each dolphin had a different repertoire, and they were trained separately, though they could watch one another through a gate.

At one performance something was clearly wrong—each animal did everything she was asked to do, but with great agitation and sometimes in the wrong sequence. Pryor confessed her puzzlement to the audience and was pleased when the show concluded successfully. Afterward her assistant said, "Do you know what happened?"

"No."

"We got the animals mixed up. Someone put Malia in Hou's holding tank and Hou in Malia's holding tank. They look so much alike now, I just never thought of that."

Each dolphin had performed the other's act, with no prior

training, having only observed it in the earlier sessions. Hou had duplicated tricks that Malia herself had invented, an upside-down jump, a corkscrew, and coasting with her tail in the air, and Malia, wearing a blindfold, had retrieved three sinking rings in a sonar demonstration. Hou had jumped through a hoop held 6 feet above the water, a feat that normally requires weeks to train.

"I stopped the departing audience and told them what they had just seen," Pryor wrote later. "I'm not sure how many understood or believed it. I still hardly believe it myself."

• • •

NEWCOMB'S PARADOX

Flamdor McSqueem is a superintelligent wombat from the planet Zortag. He shows you two boxes. You can choose to take the contents of Box A or the contents of both boxes. He has privately predicted what you will do.

If Flamdor predicted you would choose Box A only, then Box A contains $1 million. If he predicted you'd choose both boxes, then Box A contains nothing. Either way, Box B contains $1,000. What should you do?

Some people reason that Flamdor is very intelligent and his predictions are usually accurate, so it would seem best to choose Box A. Others note that Flamdor has already made his prediction and can't change the contents of the boxes now, so it seems best to take both boxes.

There's no correct answer—decision theorists are still arguing about it. What would you do?

• • •

UNSELFISH

Autological words describe themselves:

- *pentasyllabic*
- *adjectival*
- *descriptive*
- *uninformative*
- *English*
- *pronounceable*
- *confusionful*
- *wee*

Heterological words don't:

- *abbreviated*
- *adverb*
- *purple*
- *carcinogenic*
- *plural*
- *phonetic*
- *misspelled*

Is *heterological* a heterological word?

• • •

ORDER AND CHAOS

Arrange a deck of cards in alternating colors, black and red. Now cut the deck so that the bottom card of one pile is black and the other is red. Riffle-shuffle the two piles together again. Now remove cards from the top of the pack in pairs. How many of these pairs should we expect to contain cards of differing colors?

Surprisingly, all of them will. During the shuffle, suppose a black card falls first. It must be followed by either the next card in its own pile, which is red, or the first card from the other pile, which is also red. Either way, this first pair will contain one black card and one red card, and by the same principle so will each of the other 25 pairs produced by the shuffle. This effect was first identified by mathematician Norman Gilbreath in 1958.

Related: Arrange the deck in a repeating cycle of suits, such as spade-heart-club-diamond, spade-heart-club-diamond, etc. Ranks don't matter. Now deal about half of this deck onto the table and riffle-shuffle the two halves back together. If you draw cards from the top in groups of four, you'll find that each quartet contains one card of each suit.

● ● ●

A BLIND AYE

Rep. Tom Moore was dismayed at how often his colleagues in the Texas House of Representatives passed bills without understanding them. So in April 1971 he sponsored a resolution honoring Albert de Salvo:

 This compassionate gentleman's dedication and devotion to his work has enabled the weak and the lonely throughout the nation to achieve and maintain a new degree of concern for their future. He has been officially recognized by the state of Massachusetts for his noted activities and unconventional techniques involving population control and applied psychology.

That's true as far as it goes—Albert de Salvo is the Boston Strangler.

The measure passed unanimously.

•••

IMMORTAL TRUTH

In *Scripta Mathematica*, March 1955, Pedro A. Pisa offers an un-killably valid equation:

$$123789 + 561945 + 642864 = 242868 + 323787 + 761943$$

Hack away at its terms, from either end, and it remains true:

```
1      + 5      + 6      = 2      + 3      + 7
12     + 56     + 64     = 24     + 32     + 76
123    + 561    + 642    = 242    + 323    + 761
1237   + 5619   + 6428   = 2428   + 3237   + 7619
12378  + 56194  + 64286  = 24286  + 32378  + 76194
123789 + 561945 + 642864 = 242868 + 323787 + 761943
 23789 +  61945 +  42864 =  42868 +  23787 +  61943
  3789 +   1945 +   2864 =   2868 +   3787 +   1943
   789 +    945 +    864 =    868 +    787 +    943
    89 +     45 +     64 =     68 +     87 +      43
     9 +      5 +      4 =      8 +      7 +       3
```

Stab it in the heart, removing the two center digits from each term, and it still balances:

$$1289 + 5645 + 6464 = 2468 + 3287 + 7643$$

Do this again and it *still* balances:

$$19 + 55 + 64 = 28 + 37 + 73$$

Most amazing: You can square every term above, in every equation, and they'll all remain true.

• • •

"ENIGMATICAL PROPHECIES"

In his almanac, Ben Franklin made some alarming predictions for the year 1736: He said that the sea would rise and put New York and Boston under water, and that American vessels would be taken out of port "by a power with which we are not now at war."

A year later he announced he'd been right: Seawater evaporates and descends as rain, and we are not at war with the wind.

PART FOUR

EDDIE CANTOR,
the EIFFEL TOWER,
and SIR WALTER RALEIGH

ESCORT

Hit by antiaircraft fire over Bremen on Dec. 20, 1943, Air Force pilot Charlie Brown was separated from his formation. His B-17 had three damaged engines, a wounded crew, and malfunctioning electrical, hydraulic, and oxygen systems. Brown lost consciousness briefly and awoke to find himself shadowed by a German Messerschmitt that did not attack—as Brown flew slowly back to England, the enemy plane accompanied him as far as the North Sea, where the pilot saluted and let him go.

Brown returned to his air base in England, completed his tour, and returned to the United States. In the 1980s he began a search for the German pilot who had spared him, and eventually was contacted by Franz Stigler, who described the escort and the salute just as Brown had remembered them. Stigler was now living in Canada, and the two became close friends until their deaths in 2008.

Asked why he hadn't fired on Brown's shattered bomber, Stigler said, "I looked across at the tail gunner and all I could see was blood running down his gun barrels. I could see into Brown's plane, see through the holes, see how they were all shot up. They were trying to help each other. To me, it was just like they were in a parachute. I saw them and I couldn't shoot them down."

He recalled the words of his commanding officer: "You follow the rules of war for you—not your enemy. You fight by rules to keep your humanity."

• • •

ALL RELATIVE

Eddie Cantor and George Jessel played on the same bill on the vaudeville circuit.

In one town Jessel noticed that the billing read EDDIE CANTOR WITH GEORGIE JESSEL.

"What kind of conjunction is that?" he asked manager Irving Mansfield. "Eddie Cantor *with* Georgie Jessel?" Mansfield promised to fix it.

The next day the marquee read EDDIE CANTOR BUT GEORGIE JESSEL.

• • •

SMALL WORLD

"Formosa" is both a province in Argentina and the former name of Taiwan.

Curiously, those locations are on precisely opposite sides of the earth. Noon at one is midnight at the other, and midwinter at one is midsummer at the other.

• • •

UNQUOTE

"If at first you don't succeed, try, try again. Then
give up. No use being a damned fool about it."

—W.C. Fields

• • •

HOPE SPRINGS ETERNAL

Too much optimism is a bad thing. In 1897, Swedish engineer S.A. Andrée planned to reach the North Pole in a leaky and untested balloon, steering only by dragging ropes. He and two companions lifted off from Svalbard in July, drifted north and disappeared for 33 years.

It wasn't until 1930 that their last camp was discovered—they had crashed after only two days and spent three freezing months trying to walk home.

"Morale remains good," Andrée had written before his diary became incoherent. "With such comrades as these, one ought to be able to manage under practically any circumstances whatsoever."

• • •

ONE OF A KIND

You're about to roll five regular dice. Which is more likely, rolling no sixes or rolling exactly one six?

(See Answers and Solutions)

• • •

U.S. CAMEL CORPS

Necessity is the mother of invention. In the 1840s, when Army horses and mules were failing in the American Southwest, Secretary of War Jefferson Davis allocated $30,000 for "the purchase of camels and the importation of dromedaries, to be employed for military purposes." The Navy sent a ship to North Africa, and in 1856 33 confused camels arrived in Indianola, Texas.

They did pretty well. After a survey expedition to California, an enthusiastic Col. Edward Beale declared, "I look forward to the day when every mail route across the continent will be conducted . . .with this economical and noble brute."

The Civil War put an end to the project, but there's a strange postscript. Some of the camels escaped into the Texas desert, where apparently they adapted to life in the wild. The last feral camel was sighted in 1941. There's a movie in here somewhere.

• • •

"AN ORTHOGRAPHIC LAMENT"

If an S and an I and an O and a U
With an X at the end spell Su;
And an E and a Y and an E spell I,
Pray what is a speller to do?

Then, if also an S and an I and a G
And an HED spell side,
There's nothing much left for a speller to do
But to go and commit siouxeyesighed.

— Charles Follen Adams

• • •

SHIPSHAPE

The captain of a freighter was notoriously strict. On one occasion the new first mate, whom he had just hired, became a bit too boisterous after hours, and the captain wrote in the ship's log, "The first mate was drunk last night."

The mate was an able, conscientious seaman, and he pleaded

with the captain to strike this from the record. He had never been drunk before, he did his job faithfully, and he was off duty when the offense happened. He begged for leniency, pointing out that such a record would cloud his whole future.

"I can't help it," the captain said. "You were drunk last night, and I can't change the fact. The record must stand."

Wounded, the mate returned to his duties, and he stood the watch that night without complaint. In the morning he wrote in the log, "The captain was sober last night."

• • •

AN ARTIFICIAL AURORA

Karl Selim Lemström worked a quiet miracle in 1882: He strung conducting wire over the summit of a Lapland mountain and watched it draw down a shaft of light from the night sky—poetic proof that the aurora borealis is an electrical discharge from the upper atmosphere.

• • •

BETTER LATE. . .

Shizo Kanakuri disappeared while running the marathon in the 1912 Summer Olympics in Stockholm. He was listed as a missing person in Sweden for 50 years—until a journalist found him living quietly in southern Japan.

Overcome with heat during the race, he had stopped at a garden party to drink orange juice, stayed for an hour, then took a train to a hotel and sailed home the next day, too ashamed to tell anyone he was leaving.

There's a happy ending: In 1966 Kanakuri accepted an invitation to return to Stockholm and complete his run. His final time was 54 years, 8 months, 6 days, 8 hours, 32 minutes and 20.3 seconds. "It was a long trip," he said. "Along the way, I got married, had six children and 10 grandchildren."

• • •

EASY MONEY

Victor Lustig sold the Eiffel Tower for scrap—twice.

The tower was built for the Paris Exhibition of 1889, and by 1925 its upkeep was becoming a burden. So Lustig posed as a government official and summoned six scrap dealers to a secret meeting, where he told them the city wanted to dismantle it. He led a convincing tour of the site, and even induced one eager dealer to "bribe" him for the job.

Lustig fled to Vienna with the cash, and the embarrassed scrap dealer never called the cops. So the con man came back six months later and ran the same scam again, with six new dealers. This time the suspicious mark went to the police—but Lustig still escaped.

• • •

MIRROR YEARS

If you're over 23, you've lived through two years whose dates are palindromes: 1991 and 2002. That's a rare privilege. Since 1001, the normal gap between palindromic years has been 110 years (e.g., 1661-1771). The 11-year gap 1991-2002 has been the only exception, and we'll wait a millennium for the next such gap, 2992-3003. Until then we're back to 110-year intervals, and most people will see only one palindrome in a lifetime.

• • •

POSER

Q: What is the difference between a rhododendron and a cold apple-dumpling?

A: The one is a rhododendron and the other is a cold apple-dumpling.

— Angelo Lewis, *Drawing-Room Amusements*, 1879

He adds, "You surely wouldn't wish for a greater difference than that."

• • •

ONE MEAN PLANE

In 1943, after a mission in Italy, the American bomber *Lady Be Good* failed to return to its Libyan base. Apparently lost, the crew had called in for a bearing, but they never arrived. Eventually they were presumed to have crashed in the Mediterranean.

Almost 16 years later, in 1958, a team of British geologists found the plane's wreckage hundreds of miles away in the Sahara, broken in two but mysteriously well preserved. That created a second mystery: Where were the crew?

Seven bodies were eventually found, far to the north. Low on fuel and thinking themselves over the sea, they had bailed out, landed in the desert, and watched as the unmanned bomber flew out of sight carrying supplies, water, and a working radio. Amazingly, they had stayed alive for eight days in the desert; one walked 109 miles before succumbing.

The plane's mischief continued even after its destruction. When salvaged parts from the *Lady Be Good* were installed in other aircraft, they seemed to convey an odd curse. Some transmitters went into a C-54; it encountered propeller trouble and the crew saved themselves only by throwing cargo overboard. A radio receiver went into a C-47; it ditched in the Mediterranean. And an armrest went into a U.S. Army "Otter" airplane; it crashed into the Gulf of Sidra. The crew were never found, but the armrest washed quietly ashore.

• • •

REFERENCE WORK

No one knows who compiled the index for George Mivart's 1889 book *The Origin of Human Reason*, but apparently he had strong opinions. On page 136 Mivart describes a certain cockatoo that seemed to reply articulately to questions. The indexer made these entries:

> Absurd tale about a Cockatoo, 136
> Anecdote, absurd one, about a Cockatoo, 136
> Bathos and a Cockatoo, 136
> Cockatoo, absurd tale concerning one, 136
> Discourse held with a Cockatoo, 136

The same index contains entries for "Opening of oysters by monkeys" and "Dough, parrot up to its knees in." Perhaps the man was just very thorough.

• • •

THE PARADOX OF UNSUCCESSFUL INTERVENTION

Mike is overweight. His wife has just baked a cake. Happily, Mike has a box that will quiet his desire for cake. Unhappily, its battery is dead. Mike pushes the button, nothing happens, and he eats the cake.

Now, the fact that he pushed the button shows that his desire to avoid cake was greater than his desire to eat cake. So why did he push the button?

• • •

CONFLICT OF INTEREST

Eric Temple Bell led two lives. By day he was a mathematician at Caltech; by night he wrote science fiction as John Taine.

By a happy chance the two personalities met in 1951, when

the *Pasadena Star-News* asked Taine to review Bell's book *Mathematics, Queen and Servant of Science*.

Not one to lose an opportunity, he accepted. "The last flap of the jacket says Bell 'is perhaps mathematics' greatest interpreter,'" Taine wrote. "Knowing the author well, the reviewer agrees."

• • •

ROOM SERVICE

On Dec. 9, 1873, something strange happened to Thomas B. Cumpston and his wife in Bristol's Victoria Hotel. From the London *Times* of Dec. 11:

 They were alarmed at about four o'clock in the morning by terrible noises which they could not explain, and which frightened them very much. The bed seemed to open, and did all sorts of strange things. The floor, too, opened, and they heard voices. They were so terrified that they opened their bed-room window and leapt out. Mrs. Cumpston, also, gave her version of the affair. She said they heard terrible noises at about four o'clock in the morning. The floor seemed to be giving way. It certainly opened, and her husband fell down some distance, and she tried to get him up. What they said was repeated every time they spoke. Being very much frightened she asked her husband to fire off his pistol, which he did, into the ceiling.

The two leapt into the yard and ran to a nearby railway station, where police charged them with disorderly conduct and letting off firearms and released them into the custody of a friend. "No explanation can be given of this strange affair, and the belief is that it was an hallucination on the part of the husband."

• • •

UPTIME

One of Robert Benchley's movie shorts required that he be suspended above a street in a tangle of telephone wires.

While waiting for the camera, he said to his wife, "Remember how good at Latin I was in school?"

"Yes."

"Well, look where it got me."

• • •

THE "MIRACLE GIRL"

On July 25, 1956, 14-year-old Linda Morgan was in her cabin on the *Andrea Doria* when it collided with the *Stockholm* in the North Atlantic. It was feared she had been killed in the disaster: She did not reach any rescue ship, and the *Andrea Doria* capsized and sank the next morning.

But then a strange story emerged. Shortly after the collision, a crewman on the *Stockholm* had heard a young girl calling for her mother from behind a bulwark. "I was on the *Andrea Doria*," she told him. "Where am I now?"

Apparently the collision had flung her out of her bed and into the other ship. She suffered only a broken arm.

• • •

THE ROYAL SCAM

Sir Walter Raleigh once made a wager with Elizabeth that he could weigh the smoke from his tobacco pipe.

When she accepted, he weighed his tobacco, smoked the pipe, and then weighed the ashes that remained.

The queen paid him. "I have seen many a man turn his gold

into smoke," she said, "but you are the first who has turned his smoke into gold."

• • •

A PRETTY FACT

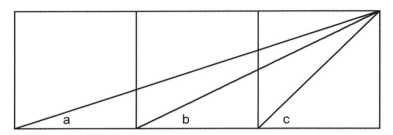

Given three adjacent squares,

$a + b = c.$

"Beauty is the first test," wrote G.H. Hardy. "There is no permanent place in the world for ugly mathematics."

• • •

SELF-HELP

Benjamin Franklin's "13 virtues," which he devised for "the bold and arduous project of arriving at moral perfection":

1. TEMPERANCE. Eat not to dullness; drink not to elevation.
2. SILENCE. Speak not but what may benefit others or yourself; avoid trifling conversation.
3. ORDER. Let all your things have their places; let each part of your business have its time.
4. RESOLUTION. Resolve to perform what you ought; perform without fail what you resolve.

5. FRUGALITY. Make no expense but to do good to others or yourself; i.e., waste nothing.

6. INDUSTRY. Lose no time; be always employ'd in something useful; cut off all unnecessary actions.

7. SINCERITY. Use no hurtful deceit; think innocently and justly, and, if you speak, speak accordingly.

8. JUSTICE. Wrong none by doing injuries, or omitting the benefits that are your duty.

9. MODERATION. Avoid extreams; forbear resenting injuries so much as you think they deserve.

10. CLEANLINESS. Tolerate no uncleanliness in body, cloaths, or habitation.

11. TRANQUILLITY. Be not disturbed at trifles, or at accidents common or unavoidable.

12. CHASTITY. Rarely use venery but for health or offspring, never to dullness, weakness, or the injury of your own or another's peace or reputation.

13. HUMILITY. Imitate Jesus and Socrates.

"It may be well my posterity should be informed that to this little artifice, with the blessing of God, their ancestor ow'd the constant felicity of his life, down to his 79th year, in which this is written."

• • •

BENARDETE'S PARADOX

Prometheus angers Zeus, who dispatches an army of demons with these instructions:

- Demon 1: If Prometheus is not dead in one hour, kill him.
- Demon 2: If Prometheus is not dead in half an hour, kill him.

• Demon 3: If Prometheus is not dead in a quarter of an hour, kill him.

And so on. When Prometheus is found dead, the council of gods is displeased, but they find it impossible to identify the guilty demon—any suspect can point to an infinity of demons who must have acted before him. Must Zeus go free?

• • •

READ IT ALOUD

An Arab came to the river side,
With a donkey bearing an obelisk;
But he would not try to ford the tide,
For he had too good an *.

— *Boston Globe*, quoted in Carolyn Wells,
A Whimsey Anthology, 1906

• • •

LAW AND ORDER

Niels Bohr liked westerns but found them exasperating. After one feature he told his friends, "I did not like that picture, it was too improbable. That the scoundrel runs off with the beautiful girl is logical, it always happens. That the bridge collapses under their carriage is unlikely but I am willing to accept it. That the heroine remains suspended in midair over a precipice is even more unlikely, but again I accept it. I am even willing to accept that at that very moment Tom Mix is coming by on his horse. But that at that very moment there should be a fellow with a motion picture camera to film the whole business—that is more than I am willing to believe."

He did approve of movie gunfights, where the villain always draws first and yet the hero always wins. Bohr reasoned that the man who draws first in a gunfight is using conscious volition, where his opponent is relying on reflex, a much faster response. Hence the second man should win.

"We disagreed with this theory," wrote George Gamow, "and the next day I went to a toy store and bought two guns in Western holsters. We shot it out with Bohr, he playing the hero, and he 'killed' all his students."

• • •

FOOD FOR THOUGHT

A force of 1 newton is about the weight of an apple.

• • •

FATHOMLESS GENIUS

On Aug. 11, 1966, a fishing boat came upon a badly bruised man floating in the water off Brest, France, clutching an inflatable life raft. He identified himself as Josef Papp, a Hungarian-Canadian engineer, and claimed he had just bailed out of a jet-powered submarine that had crossed the Atlantic in 13 hours.

The media laughed at this, but Papp insisted he had built a cone-shaped sub in his garage that could reach 300 mph using the same principle as a supercavitating torpedo. He even wrote a book, *The Fastest Submarine*, to answer his critics . . .but somehow this failed to explain how the sub worked, or why plane tickets to France had been found in his pocket, or why a man matching his description had been seen boarding a plane to France hours earlier.

For what it's worth, Papp did patent a number of other inventions, including a fuel mixture composed from inert noble gases. So maybe he was telling the truth.

• • •

"STRENGTH AND SAGACITY OF A FOX"

66 In 1815, a fox was caught in a trap, at Bourne, Cambridgeshire, with which he made off. He was traced in the snow the following morning, by the Earl of De La Warr's gamekeeper, upwards of ten miles, and was taken out of the earth alive and strong. His pad was then in the trap, which, with three feet of chain at the end of it, is supposed to have weighed fourteen pounds. Another fox accompanied him the whole of the way, seldom being distant from him more than four or five yards.

— *The Cabinet of Curiosities*, 1824

• • •

HOMEWORK

One day while teaching a class at Yale, mathematician Shizuo Kakutani wrote a lemma on the blackboard and remarked that the proof was obvious. A student timidly raised his hand and said that it wasn't obvious to him. Kakutani stared at the lemma for some moments and realized that he couldn't prove it himself. He apologized and said he would report back at the next class meeting.

After class he went straight to his office and worked for some time further on the proof. Still unsuccessful, he skipped lunch, went to the library, and tracked down the original paper. It stated the lemma clearly but left the proof as an "exercise for the reader." The author was Shizuo Kakutani.

• • •

MIND GAMES

- Déjà vu—the feeling of having seen an unfamiliar thing previously
- Déjà vécu—the feeling of having experienced an unfamiliar situation previously
- Déjà visité—unaccountable knowledge of an unfamiliar place
- Déjà senti—a sense of "recollection" of an unfamiliar idea
- Jamais vu—a sense of unfamiliarity with a familiar situation
- Presque vu—inability to summon a familiar word

Visiting a ruined English manor in 1856, Nathaniel Hawthorne felt "haunted and perplexed" by the idea that he had seen it before. He realized later that Alexander Pope had written a poem about it nearly 100 years earlier.

• • •

LONG STORY

Between the 762nd and 767th decimal places of pi there are six 9s in a row.

It's called the Feynman point, because physicist Richard Feynman said he'd like to recite 761 digits and end with "...nine, nine, nine, nine, nine, nine, and so on."

• • •

RIMSHOT

66 A moving Sermon being preached in a Country Church, all fell a weeping but one Man, who being ask'd, Why he did not weep with the rest? Oh! said he, I belong to another parish.

— *The Jester's Magazine*, November 1766

• • •

ROUND TRIP

A man eats breakfast at his camp, then travels due south. After going 10 miles in a straight line he stops for lunch. Then he sets out again due south. After going 10 miles in a straight line he finds himself back at camp. Where is he?

(See Answers and Solutions)

• • •

GOOD BOY

In 1924, university professor Hidesamuro Ueno brought his dog, Hachiko, to Tokyo. Every morning Hachiko saw his master off at the front door, and every evening he greeted him at the nearby train station.

The professor died in May 1925, but the faithful dog still went to the station every day to wait for him.

He kept this up for nine years.

The dog became a national sensation in 1932, when this story was published, and he's since been the subject of books and movies. Today a bronze statue stands at Shibuya Station, where he kept his vigil.

• • •

BEWITCHED

What's remarkable about these numbers?

```
 1/19 = .0 5 2 6 3 1 5 7 8 9 4 7 3 6 8 4 2 1 ...
 2/19 = .1 0 5 2 6 3 1 5 7 8 9 4 7 3 6 8 4 2 ...
 3/19 = .1 5 7 8 9 4 7 3 6 8 4 2 1 0 5 2 6 3 ...
 4/19 = .2 1 0 5 2 6 3 1 5 7 8 9 4 7 3 6 8 4 ...
 5/19 = .2 6 3 1 5 7 8 9 4 7 3 6 8 4 2 1 0 5 ...
 6/19 = .3 1 5 7 8 9 4 7 3 6 8 4 2 1 0 5 2 6 ...
 7/19 = .3 6 8 4 2 1 0 5 2 6 3 1 5 7 8 9 4 7 ...
 8/19 = .4 2 1 0 5 2 6 3 1 5 7 8 9 4 7 3 6 8 ...
 9/19 = .4 7 3 6 8 4 2 1 0 5 2 6 3 1 5 7 8 9 ...
10/19 = .5 2 6 3 1 5 7 8 9 4 7 3 6 8 4 2 1 0 ...
11/19 = .5 7 8 9 4 7 3 6 8 4 2 1 0 5 2 6 3 1 ...
12/19 = .6 3 1 5 7 8 9 4 7 3 6 8 4 2 1 0 5 2 ...
13/19 = .6 8 4 2 1 0 5 2 6 3 1 5 7 8 9 4 7 3 ...
14/19 = .7 3 6 8 4 2 1 0 5 2 6 3 1 5 7 8 9 4 ...
15/19 = .7 8 9 4 7 3 6 8 4 2 1 0 5 2 6 3 1 5 ...
16/19 = .8 4 2 1 0 5 2 6 3 1 5 7 8 9 4 7 3 6 ...
17/19 = .8 9 4 7 3 6 8 4 2 1 0 5 2 6 3 1 5 7 ...
18/19 = .9 4 7 3 6 8 4 2 1 0 5 2 6 3 1 5 7 8 ...
```

They form a perfect magic square. Each row, column, and diagonal adds to 81.

Engineer W.S. Andrews wrote, "Considering its constructive origin and interesting features, this square, notwithstanding its simplicity, may be fairly said to present one of the most remarkable illustrations of the intrinsic harmony of numbers."

• • •

"GET THEE BEHIND ME"

Here's one way to beat temptation: file a lawsuit. In 1971, Gerald Mayo sued "Satan and his staff" in U.S. District Court for the Western District of Pennsylvania. He alleged that "Satan has on numerous occasions caused plaintiff misery and unwarranted threats, against the will of plaintiff, that Satan has placed deliberate obstacles in his path and has caused plaintiff's downfall" and had therefore "deprived him of his constitutional rights," a violation of the U.S. Code.

The court noted that jurisdiction was uncertain; legally the devil might count as a foreign prince. Also, Mayo's claim seemed appropriate for a class action suit, and it wasn't clear that Mayo could represent all of humanity. Finally, no one was sure how the U.S. Marshal could serve process on Satan.

So the devil got away. Mayo's case has been cited several times, and has never been overturned or contradicted.

• • •

THE MEASURE OF A MAN

One "smoot" is five feet seven inches, or about 1.7 meters.

It's named for Oliver R. Smoot, an ill-starred MIT pledge whose fraternity brothers used him as a human yardstick to measure the Harvard Bridge in October 1958.

The bridge measured "364.4 smoots plus one ear." The markings are repainted each year by the incoming pledge class of Lambda Chi Alpha.

Ironically, Smoot later became chairman of the American National Standards Institute.

• • •

IN A WORD

spanghew
v. to launch a frog or toad into the air

whelve
v. to cover with an inverted bowl

bemissionary
v. to annoy with missionaries

unasinous
adj. equally stupid

• • •

FREE WILL

I suppose I could try if I chose,
But the question is: "Can I suppose
I could choose what I chose if
I chose?" I suppose if
I chose to. But nobody knows.

— Anonymous

• • •

A MARTIAN CENSUS

A room contains more than one Martian. Each Martian has two
hands, with at least one finger on each hand, and all Martians

have the same number of fingers. Altogether there are between 200 and 300 Martian fingers in the room; if you knew the exact number, you could deduce the exact number of Martians. How many Martians are there, and how many fingers does each one have?

(See Answers and Solutions)

• • •

AGITATO

" A fight with a piano that came near proving disastrous to the greatest of pianists, occurred on shipboard while Paderewski was on his way to New York a short time ago. Paderewski in his state room had a small upright piano on which to practice. It was fastened to the floor by means of bolts. On the opposite side of the room was the bed. In a heavy storm the piano was loosened by the rolling of the vessel. Straight it made for the pianist and crashed into his bed, nearly pinning him to the wall. Paderewski on reaching the floor rushed to the opposite side of the room. Instantly the piano followed, coming at him with great force. He dodged it, but it came at him again, being hurled about in the room by the rolling of the boat. The pianist tried to get out the door, but could not loosen the bolt and he was thus hemmed in with the tumbling piano which threatened to crush him to death at every second. There was nothing to do but wrestle with the instrument. He grasped it as it came toward him again and after lengthy struggle in which he was nearly exhausted, succeeded in binding it to the wall.

— *Popular Mechanics*, 1902

• • •

EXIT SPEECH

When New York gangster Dutch Schultz was shot in 1935, police had a stenographer take down his delirious last words. Find a confession here if you can:

- "Police, police, Henry and Frankie. Oh, oh, dog biscuits and when he is happy he doesn't get snappy."
- "I am a pretty good pretzler. Winifred. Department of Justice. I even get it from the department."
- "Please, I had nothing with him. He was a cowboy in one of the seven-days-a-week fight."
- "There are only 10 of us. There are 10 million fighting somewhere of you, so get your onions up and we will throw up the truce flag."
- "The sidewalk was in trouble and the bears were in trouble and I broke it up."
- "No payrolls, no walls, no coupons. That would be entirely out."
- "Oh, sir, get the doll a roofing."
- "A boy has never wept nor dashed a thousand kim. Did you hear me?"
- "Please put me up on my feet at once. You are a hard-boiled man. Did you hear me?"
- "Please crack down on the Chinaman's friends and Hitler's commander. I am sure and I am going up and I am going to give you honey if I can."
- "I am half crazy. They won't let me get up. They dyed my shoes. Open those shoes. Give me something. I am so sick."

His final words were "I will settle the indictment. Come on, open the soap duckets. The chimney sweeps. Talk to the sword. Shut up, you got a big mouth! Please help me up, Henry. Max, come over here. French-Canadian bean soup. I want to pay. Let them leave me alone."

PART FIVE

STARLINGS, LENTILS, *and* SHERLOCK HOLMES

THE TOMAHAWK STORY

When Alec Guinness was filming *The Swan* in North Carolina in 1955, someone gave him a tomahawk purchased at a local fairground. Guinness thought it too heavy to take with him, so as he was departing he paid a porter to slip it into Grace Kelly's bed.

Years later, while performing in London, he found the tomahawk in his own bed.

This meant war. Guinness bided his time until the princess visited America on a poetry tour; then he contacted the English actor with whom she was traveling and persuaded him to leave the tomahawk in her bed. ("Do you know Alec Guinness?" she asked him the next day. "No, I've never met him," he said.)

Guinness thought no more about it until 1980, when he visited Hollywood to accept an honorary Oscar and found the tomahawk in his hotel bed. He waited until Kelly's next tour of England and arranged to have it left in her suitcase.

She died in 1982, so that was the last laugh. There was no one to share it with—in 25 years, neither of them had ever acknowledged that this was happening.

• • •

TRIPLE VISION

EYE is a palindrome in English, Spanish (OJO), and Polish (OKO).

• • •

NEXT STOP . . .

If Hélène Smith wasn't a real psychic, she was a remarkably ambitious fake—she claimed to be able to visit Mars:

 How funny, these cars! Hardly any horses or people that are on the move. Imagine different kinds of armchairs that slide but don't have wheels. It is the tiny wheels that produce the sparks. People sit in their armchairs. Some of them, the larger ones, hold four to five people. To the right of the armchairs a kind of handle stick is attached, fitted with a button that one presses with the thumb to put the vehicle in motion. There are no rails. One also sees the people walking. They are built like us and hold onto each other with the little finger. The clothing is the same for both sexes: a long blouse tight around the waist, very large trousers, shoes with very thick soles, no heel and of the same colour as the rest of the outfit which is in shammy, white with black designs.

Between 1894 and 1901 she gave 60 séances, detailing the Martian language and eventually inspiring a book, *From India to the Planet Mars*, by University of Geneva psychologist Theodor Flournoy.

Matisse wrote, "There are always flowers for those who want to see them."

• • •

MEMORABLE INDEXES

From Henry Wheatley's index to Samuel Pepys' diary:

Periwig, Pepys wears one, iii. 116, 327; Pepys puts off the wearing of one for a while, iii. 265; one bought by Pepys, iii. 323; he buys a case for it, iii. 328; Pepys so altered by it that the Duke of York did not know him, iii. 334; Pepys has a second made of his own hair, iii. 341, 342; he sends one to the barber's to be cleansed of its nits, iv. 190; he buys two more, vi. 245; Pepys agrees with a barber to keep his in order, viii. 33; his, set on fire, viii. 118; King and Duke of York first wear periwigs, iv. 43; danger of wearing periwigs during the Plague, v. 64; Ladies of Honour in, v. 324; periwig shops, iii. 116, 316, 326; vi. 314; viii. 127.

From James Russell Lowell's index to *The Biglow Papers*:

Alligator, a decent one conjectured to be, in some sort, humane, 156

Birch, virtue of, in instilling certain of the dead languages, 134

Christian soldiers, perhaps inconsistent, whether, 64

Eating words, habit of, convenient in time of famine, 76

Epaulets, perhaps no badge of saintship, 55

Fire, we all like to play with it, 85

National pudding, its effect on the organs of speech, a curious physiological fact, 51

Paris, liberal principles safe as far away as, 96

People soft enough, 98—want correct ideas, 131

Pleiades, the, not enough esteemed, 103

Present, not long wonderful, 103

Riches conjectured to have legs as well as wings, 92

Satan, never wants attorneys, 48

Speech-making, an abuse of gift of speech, 81

Venetians, invented something once, 135

From Lewis Carroll's index to *Sylvie and Bruno*:

Crocodiles, logic of, 230

Electricity, influence of, on Literature, 64

Frog, young, how to amuse, 364

Ghosts, treatment of, in Railway-Literature, 58

Loving or being loved. Which is best? 77

Parentheses in conversation, how to indicate, 251

Weltering, appropriate fluids for, 58

Carroll's index also includes entries for "Boots for horizontal weather," "Horizontal rain, boots for," "Rain, horizontal, boots for," and "Weather, horizontal, boots for":

"But what's the use of wearing umbrellas round one's knees?"

"In ordinary rain," the Professor admitted, "they would not be of much use. But if ever it rained horizontally, you know, they would be invaluable—simply invaluable!"

• • •

A UNIVERSAL SOLUTION

In 1965, Dmitri Borgmann noted that this expression:

$$11 + 2 - 1 = 12$$

. . .is valid also when interpreted as a set of characters:

$$11 \text{ "+ 2"} = 112; 112 \text{ "- 1"} = 12$$

. . .as a set of Roman numerals:

$$XI + II = XIII; XIII - I = XII$$

. . .and even as a set of letters:

ELEVEN + TWO = ELEVENTWO
ELEVENTWO - ONE = LEVETW (= TWELVE)

• • •

EPISODE

Pianist Pete Brush was waiting for his wife outside a Manhattan department store when a woman with a violin case approached him and said, "How can I get to Carnegie Hall?"

He said, "Go uptown to 57th Street and make a left to 7th Avenue."

• • •

OOPS

In 1890, a well-intentioned New Yorker named Eugene Schieffelin released 80 starlings in Central Park. He wanted to introduce every bird mentioned the works of William Shakespeare into the United States. (In *The First Part of King Henry the Fourth*, Hotspur says, "Nay, I'll have a starling shall be taught to speak nothing but 'Mortimer.'")

He should have reconsidered. Scientists estimate that those birds have multiplied into more than 200 million in North America, where the starling has become a major pest, outcompeting

other birds for nest holes. Opponents of genetically modified or-
ganisms still point to Schieffelin's act to warn of the dangers of
invasive species.

• • •

AN INTIMATE MOMENT

In the 1924 silent film *Three Weeks*, Conrad Nagel tenderly picks
up Aileen Pringle to carry her into the bedroom.

Lip readers noted that she appears to be saying, "If you drop
me, you bastard, I'll break your neck."

• • •

VARYING REPORTS

Which statements on this list are true?

1. Exactly one statement on this list is false.
2. Exactly two statements on this list are false.
3. Exactly three statements on this list are false.
4. Exactly four statements on this list are false.
5. Exactly five statements on this list are false.
6. Exactly six statements on this list are false.
7. Exactly seven statements on this list are false.
8. Exactly eight statements on this list are false.
9. Exactly nine statements on this list are false.
10. Exactly ten statements on this list are false.

(See Answers and Solutions)

• • •

THE CRAWFORDSVILLE MONSTER

The *Indianapolis Journal* of Sept. 5, 1891, reports that two icemen were hitching a wagon in Crawfordsville, Ind., at 2 a.m. on Sept. 4 when they saw in the sky "a horrible apparition approaching from the west." A headless monster, 18 feet long and 8 feet wide, floated 300 feet overhead, apparently propelled by fins. It circled a nearby house, disappeared to the east, then returned, emitting a wheezing, moaning sound. The men fled, but the noise awakened a Methodist pastor, who saw the creature from his window.

Reportedly it returned on the following evening, when hundreds of witnesses saw a flapping "thing" that "squirmed in agony" and made a "wheezing, plaintive noise" as it hovered in the sky.

That's all we know. The creature, if it really existed, never returned to Crawfordsville.

• • •

FOOD FOR TOMORROW

By 1941 Russian botanist Nikolai Vavilov had created the largest seed bank in the world, a collection of 400,000 seeds, roots, and fruits whose genetic material held the future of Soviet agriculture. Unfortunately it was located in Leningrad, which Hitler encircled that summer and began to starve.

The siege of Leningrad lasted two years and cost more than a million lives, and Vavilov's scientists endured it surrounded by edible plants. "As they slowly starved, they refused to eat from any of their collection containers of rice, peas, corn and wheat," two survivors remembered in 1993. "They chose torment and death in order to preserve Vavilov's gene bank."

The collection filled 16 rooms, in which no one was allowed to remain alone. Workers stored potatoes in the basement and guarded them in shifts, "numb with cold and emaciated from hunger." Botanist Dmitri Ivanov died preserving thousands of packets of rice; peanut specialist Alexander Stchukin died at his writing table. In all, nine scientists and workers chose to die of starvation rather than eat the plants. Vavilov himself died in a labor camp in 1943, but today his bank is the world's largest collection of fruits and berries.

• • •

A LOSS FOR WORDS

In 1922, Ernest Hemingway's wife lost a suitcase full of his early manuscripts at the Gare de Lyons as she was traveling to meet him in Geneva. It was never recovered.

In 1919, T.E. Lawrence misplaced his briefcase while changing trains at Reading railway station. It had contained the first eight books of *Seven Pillars of Wisdom*. He, too, had to start again.

In 1835, when Thomas Carlyle had finished writing the first volume in his history of the French Revolution, he loaned the manuscript to John Stuart Mill, seeking his opinion. Mill's maid mistook it for trash and burned it.

"I remember and can still remember less of it than of anything I ever wrote with such toil," Carlyle wrote in his journal. After laboriously rewriting the volume, he said he felt like a man who had "nearly killed himself accomplishing zero."

• • •

AIR HAZARD

In 1973, over Ivory Coast, an aircraft collided with a Ruppell's griffon, a kind of vulture.

It had been flying at 37,000 feet—that's seven miles high.

•••

MARKETING CHALLENGE #194782

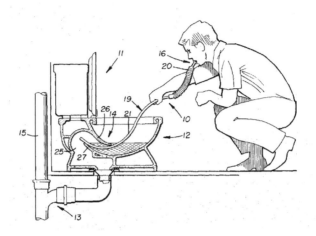

Okay, there's good news and bad news. The good news is that we've found a safe source of fresh air for people trapped in high-rise hotel fires. The bad news is that they have to feed a breathing tube into a vent pipe in the sewer line.

William Holmes' 1981 brainstorm probably would have saved many lives, but even a guest surrounded by toxic smoke has some natural squeamishness.

•••

ICE ROUTE

The largest gem-quality diamond ever found was discovered in a South African mine in 1905. The so-called Cullinan diamond weighed 3,106 carats, or about 1-1/3 pounds.

The Transvaal government purchased the stone and offered it to Edward VII on his 66th birthday, but the problem remained how to transport such a valuable object safely to England. Amid great publicity and heavy security, an ocean liner set out carefully for London.

It was carrying a decoy stone—the real diamond was sent by parcel post. It arrived safely.

•••

TRIVIUM

The highest point in the contiguous United States is less than 80 miles from the lowest point.

Mount Whitney, in California's Sequoia National Park, rises 14,505 feet above sea level.

It's 76 miles west of Badwater, in Death Valley National Park, which is 282 feet below sea level.

•••

GUYS AND DOLLS

" 'The other day,' said a man passenger, 'I saw a woman in an omnibus open a satchel and take out a purse, close the satchel and open the purse, take out a penny and close the purse, open the satchel and put in the purse. Then she gave the penny to the conductor and took a halfpenny in exchange. Then she opened the satchel and took out the purse, closed the satchel and opened the purse, put in the halfpenny and closed the purse, opened the satchel and put in the purse, closed the satchel and locked both ends.

Then she felt to see if her back hair was all right, and it was all right, and she was all right. That was a woman.'

— *The Windsor Magazine*, November 1907

It is necessary for technical reasons that these warheads be stored upside down; that is, with the top at the bottom and the bottom at the top. In order that there may be no doubt as to which is the bottom and which is the top, it will be seen to that the bottom of each warhead immediately be labelled with the word TOP.

— British Admiralty, quoted in *Applied Optics*, January 1968

• • •

CREDENTIALS

When Steven Spielberg dropped out of college in 1968, he was only a few credits short of a diploma.

So in 2002, after winning three Oscars, five honorary doctorates, and two lifetime achievement awards, he returned to California State University, Long Beach, to complete a degree in film and electronic arts.

He placed out of FEA 309, the advanced filmmaking class. To demonstrate his proficiency, he submitted *Schindler's List.*

• • •

NEVERMORE

Edgar Allan Poe's poem "The Raven" does not contain the letter Z.

• • •

CUT!

Director Curtis Bernhardt was midway through shooting *My Reputation* in 1944 when he encountered some trouble with one of the stars. Robert Archer insisted on wearing a jacket and shirt while mowing a lawn under the hot California sun.

Bernhardt pressed him, and to his surprise Archer said, "Okay, okay, I'm a girl."

She was Tanis Chandler, a 20-year-old typist in a local brokerage office who'd gotten tired of waiting for acting jobs. Posing as Archer, she'd won a part in 1943's *The Desert Song*, where robes and a burnoose had hid her shape. She'd done so well that the casting office had sent her out for Bernhardt's film.

"The studios are always yelling about the lack of men," she said. "I thought I'd have better luck in male roles. Oh, well."

• • •

TIDY

FORTY is the only number whose letters appear in alphabetical order.

• • •

LETTER SHIFT

YZABCDEFGHIJKLMNO
EFGHIJKLMNOPQRSTU
STUVWXYZABCDEFGHI

Advance each of the letters in YES 16 places through the alphabet and you get OUI, the French word for yes.

• • •

A CANDID PUZZLE

Bertrand Russell admired G.E. Moore's dedication to the truth.

"I have never but once succeeded in making him tell a lie," he wrote, "and that was by a subterfuge.

"'Moore,' I said, 'do you always speak the truth?'

"'No,' he replied.

"I believe this to be the only lie he ever told."

• • •

THE STOPPED CLOCK

Andrea's only timepiece is a clock that's fixed to the wall. One day she forgets to wind it and it stops.

She travels across town to have dinner with a friend whose own clock is always correct. When she returns home, she makes a simple calculation and sets her own clock accurately.

How does she manage this without knowing the travel time between her house and her friend's?

(See Answers and Solutions)

• • •

FAIR ENOUGH

> A prisoner being called on to plead an indictment for larceny was told by the clerk to hold up his right hand. The man immediately held up his left hand. 'Hold up your right hand,' said the clerk. 'Please your Honor,' said the culprit, still keeping up his left hand, 'I am left-handed.'

— Franklin Fiske Heard, *Oddities of the Law*, 1881

• • •

THE PRICE

Aristippus passed Diogenes as he was washing lentils.

He said, "If you could but learn to flatter the king, you would not have to live on lentils."

Diogenes said, "And if you could learn to live on lentils, you would not have to flatter the king."

• • •

COSMOPOLITAN

Denmark, Norway, Poland, Sweden, Bristol, Cambridge, Leeds, Manchester, Monmouth, Newcastle, Oxford, Plymouth, Wales, Athens, Belfast, Belgrade, Bremen, Calais, Dresden, Frankfort, Hanover, Lisbon, Madrid, Moscow, Naples, Palermo, Paris, Rome, Sorrento, Stockholm, and Vienna ...

 . . .are all towns in Maine.

• • •

TEMPTING

The Earl of Yarborough offers you a wager. He'll shuffle an ordinary deck and deal you 13 cards. If none of your cards ranks above 9, he'll give you a thousand pounds. Otherwise you must give him one pound.

Should you accept?

(See Answers and Solutions)

• • •

THE PARROT OF ATURES

In exploring the upper Orinoco around 1800, Alexander von Humboldt learned of a tribe, the Atures, that had recently died out there. Their language had died with them, but Humboldt was still able to hear it spoken: "At the period of our voyage an old parrot was shown at Maypures, of which the inhabitants related, and the fact is worthy of observation, that 'they did not understand what it said, because it spoke the language of the Atures.'" From a 19th-century poem:

> Where are now the youths who bred him
> To pronounce their mother tongue?
> Where the gentle maids who fed him
> And who built his nest when young?

Humboldt managed to record phonetically 40 words spoken by the parrot, and in 1997 artist Rachel Berwick painstakingly taught two Amazon parrots to speak them. Can a language be said to survive if no one knows its meaning?

• • •

IN A WORD

decemnovenarianize
v. to act like a person of the 19th century

unlove
v. to cease to love

gongoozler
n. an idler who stares at activity on a canal

paneity
n. the state of being bread

• • •

WORK SMARTER, NOT HARDER

On Dec. 10, 1968, a uniformed man pulled over a bank car in Tokyo. He explained that police had received a warning that dynamite had been planted in the vehicle, which was transporting bonuses for local Toshiba employees. The four passengers got out and watched as the officer crawled underneath.

After a moment he rolled out, shouting that the car was about to explode. When the passengers ran, he got in and drove off.

Thus one man stole 294,307,500 yen in broad daylight, working alone and without harming anyone. It remains the largest single heist in Japanese history. The thief was never caught.

• • •

BACKTRACKING

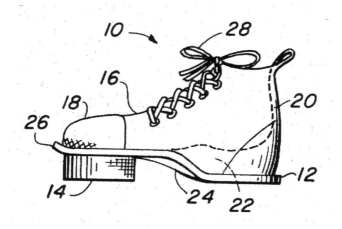

This is clever—in 1974 Cecil Slemp invented shoes with reversed soles, to leave footprints that point in the opposite direction.

So now your bloody tracks will lead *to* the murder scene.

• • •

WHAT'S THAT DOING THERE?

The integer 8 can be written as the sum of two squares of integers, $m^2 + n^2$, in four ways, when (m, n) is (2, 2), (2, -2), (-2, 2), or (-2, -2).

The integer 7 can't be written at all as the sum of such squares.

Remarkably, over a very large collection of integers from 1 to *n*, the average number of ways an integer can be written as the sum of two squares approaches π. Why should this be?

• • •

HARD BARGAINING

In Robert Louis Stevenson's story "The Bottle Imp," the titular imp will grant its owner (almost) any wish, but if the owner dies with the bottle then he burns in hell. He may sell the bottle, but he must charge less than he paid for it, and the new buyer must understand these conditions.

Now, no one would buy such a bottle for 1 cent, as he could not then sell it again. (The imp can't make you immortal, or support prices smaller than one cent, or alter the conditions.) And if 1 cent is too low a price, then so is 2 cents, for the same reason. And so on, apparently forever. It would be irrational to buy the bottle for any price.

But intuitively most people would consider $1,000 a reasonable price to pay for the use of a wish-granting genie. Who's right?

• • •

STIRRED, NOT SHAKEN

Beginning work on a new novel in 1953, Ian Fleming found himself stumped for a name for his hero, a British Secret Service agent. His eye strayed across the bookshelves of his Jamaican estate, and he found "just what I needed."

It was *Birds of the West Indies*, by James Bond.

• • •

"MONKEYS DEMANDING THEIR DEAD"

 Mr. Forbes tells a story of a female monkey (the *Semno-pithecus Entellus*) who was shot by a friend of his, and carried to his tent. Forty or fifty of her tribe advanced with menacing gestures, but stood still when the gentleman presented his gun at them. One, however, who appeared to be the chief of the tribe, came forward, chattering and threatening in a furious manner. Nothing short of firing at him seemed likely to drive him away; but at length he approached the tent door with every sign of grief and supplication, as if he were begging for the body. It was given to him, he took it in his arms, carried it away, with actions expressive of affection, to his companions, and with them disappeared. It was not to be wondered at that the sportsman vowed never to shoot another monkey.

— Edmund Fillingham King, *Ten Thousand Wonderful Things*, 1860

• • •

NEVERMORE

Seeing a red apple should increase your confidence that all ravens are black.

Why? Because the statement "All ravens are black" is logically equivalent to "All non-black things are non-ravens." And seeing a red apple (or green grass) confirms this belief.

This is logically inescapable, even if it's counterintuitive. It's known as Hempel's paradox.

• • •

SELF-HELP

Someone once asked G.K. Chesterton what book he'd most like to have on a desert island.

He answered, *"Thomas's Guide to Practical Shipbuilding."*

• • •

PICK'S THEOREM

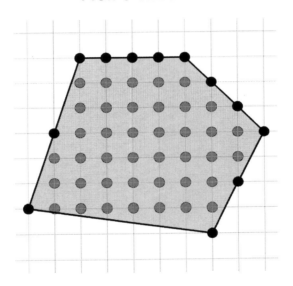

Georg Alexander Pick found a useful way to determine the area of a simple polygon with integer coordinates. If i is the number of lattice points in the interior and b is the number of lattice points on the boundary, then the area is given by

$$A = i + b/2 - 1.$$

There are 40 lattice points in the interior of the figure above and 12 on the boundary, so its area is $40 + 12/2 - 1 = 45$.

• • •

WHAT IS IT?

Here's one of the most beautiful riddles in the English language. It's commonly attributed to Byron, but it was composed in 1814 by Catherine Maria Fanshawe, the daughter of a Surrey squire:

> 'Twas whispered in heaven, 'twas muttered in hell,
> And echo caught faintly the sound as it fell;
> On the confines of earth 'twas permitted to rest,
> And the depths of the ocean its presence confessed.
> 'Twill be found in the sphere when 'tis riven asunder;
> 'Tis seen in the lightning, and heard in the thunder.
> 'Twas allotted to man from his earliest breath;
> It assists at his birth, and attends him in death;
> It presides o'er his happiness, honour, and health;
> Is the prop of his house, and the end of his wealth.
> In the heap of the miser 'tis hoarded with care,
> But is sure to be lost in his prodigal heir.
> It begins every hope, every wish it must bound,
> It prays with the hermit, with monarchs is crowned.
> Without it the soldier and seaman may roam,
> But woe to the wretch who expels it from home.
> In the whispers of conscience 'tis sure to be found;
> Nor e'en in the whirlwind of passion is drowned.
> 'Twill soften the heart, and though deaf to the ear,
> 'Twill make it acutely and constantly hear.
> But, in short, let it rest like a beautiful flower;
> Oh, breathe on it softly, it dies in an hour.

What is it?

(See Answers and Solutions)

• • •

CURIOSITIES OF MORSE CODE

- SISSIES: ··· ·· ··· ·· ·· ···
- MOTTO:-- --- - - ---
- ENTENTE: · -· - · -· ·
- TARTAR: - ·- ·- · ·- ·-·
- POSSESSIVENESS: ·--- --- ··· ··· · ··· ··· ·· ···· · ·- · ··· ··· (18 dots in a row)
- SERVOMOTOR: ··· · ·- ···- --- -- --- - --- ·- (12 dashes)

INTRANSIGENCE is a palindrome: ·· -· - ·- ·- -· ··· ·· -· · ·- · -·- ·

• • •

CONFIRMED

Abraham de Moivre correctly predicted the date of his own death.

He noted that he was sleeping 15 minutes longer each day and surmised that he would die on the day he slept for 24 hours. That date, he calculated, would be Nov. 27, 1754.

He was right.

• • •

SPIROLATERALS

Imagine you have a little robot that holds a pencil. Set it down on a sheet of paper and give it these instructions:

1. Move forward 3 units and turn right.
2. Move forward 1 unit and turn right.
3. Move forward 2 units and turn left.
4. Move forward 1 unit and turn left.

5. Move forward 2 units and turn right.

6. Repeat.

If the robot makes its turns at 90° angles, it will produce this figure:

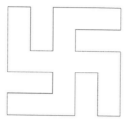

But, remarkably, if it turns at 120° it will draw this:

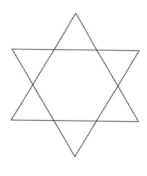

• • •

ODD DUCK

This is the opening of Chapter 4 of Mark Twain's *A Double Barrelled Detective Story*:

 It was a crisp and spicy morning in early October. The lilacs and laburnums, lit with the glory-fires of autumn, hung burning and flashing in the upper air, a fairy bridge provided by kind nature for the wingless wild things that have their home in the tree-tops and would visit together; the larch and the pomegranate flung their purple and yellow flames in brilliant broad splashes along the slanting sweep of woodland; the sensuous fragrance of innumerable deciduous flowers rose upon the swooning atmosphere; far in the empty sky a solitary oesophagus slept upon motionless wing; everywhere brooded stillness, serenity, and the peace of God.

Twain later recalled that few readers noticed anything wrong with it.

• • •

ELEMENTARY

Sherlock Holmes was based on a real man, Scottish surgeon Joseph Bell, whom Arthur Conan Doyle had served as a clerk in the Edinburgh Royal Infirmary.

Bell was famous for making deductions about his patients. He greeted one by saying, "Ah, I perceive that you are a soldier, a noncommissioned officer, and that you have served in Bermuda."

When the man acknowledged this, Bell addressed his students. "How did I know that, gentlemen? The matter is simplicity itself. He came into the room without taking his hat off, as he would go into an orderly's room. He was a soldier. A slight authoritative air, combined with his age, shows that he was a noncommissioned officer. A slight rash on the forehead tells me that he was in Bermuda, and subject to a certain rash known only there."

On another occasion Bell challenged his students to identify a bitter drug by taste alone. They watched him dip a finger into the tumbler and taste it, and reluctantly followed suit. "Gentlemen," he said with a laugh, "I am deeply grieved to find that not one of you has developed this power of perception which I so often speak about; for if you had watched me closely, you would have found that while I placed my forefinger in the medicine, it was the middle finger which found its way into my mouth."

• • •

CHECKMATE

66 When Dr. Franklin went to France on his revolutionary mission, his eminence as a philosopher, his venerable appearance, and the cause on which he was sent, rendered him extremely popular—for all ranks and conditions of men there entered warmly into the American interest. He was, therefore, feasted and invited to all the court parties. At these he sometimes met the old Duchess of Bourbon, who being a chess-player of about his force, they were very generally played together. Happening once to put her king into prise, the Doctor took it. 'Ah,' says she, 'we do not take kings so.' 'We do in America,' said the Doctor.

— Sarah Randolph, *The Domestic Life of Thomas Jefferson*, 1871

• • •

A NOISY EXIT

On Aug. 27, 1883, the sound of gunfire was reported by the coast guard on Rodrigues Island in the Indian Ocean.

It wasn't gunfire. It was the "death cry" of Krakatoa, 3,000 miles away in Indonesia—the loudest sound in recorded history.

PART SIX

ROSES, NUMBER THEORY,
and MARCUS AURELIUS

REMEMBERED

On the morning after Jack Benny died in 1974, his wife, Mary, received a single long-stemmed rose. Another arrived the next day, and the next. For the first few weeks she was too numb to wonder where they were coming from, but eventually she called the florist to inquire.

He told her that Benny had visited the shop some years earlier to send a bouquet of flowers to a friend. As he was leaving, he suddenly turned back and said, "If anything should happen to me, I want you to send Mary a single rose every day."

She continued to receive them every day until June 30, 1983—when she herself passed away.

• • •

WORTH A TRY

Publicity hound Jim Moran brought a sealed case of playing cards to a meeting of magicians. One randomly chosen audience member opened the case, a second chose a deck, a third opened the deck, a fourth cut it, and a fifth chose a card.

Moran said, "It's the six of diamonds."

It wasn't. "But if it *had* been the six of diamonds," Moran said later, "those bastards would *still* be talking about it."

• • •

NOTED

Christopher Morley named his cats Shall and Will, "because nobody can tell them apart."

• • •

LONG AND SHORT

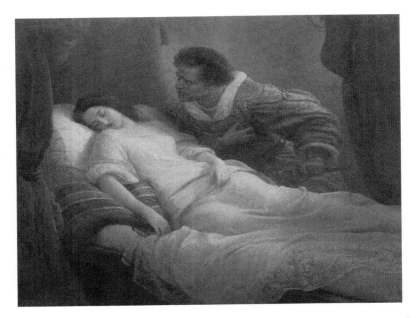

Othello doesn't fit. Act I takes place on Othello's wedding night, when he is sent to Cyprus. Act II takes place on the day of his arrival there, Acts III and IV occur together on the following day, and Act V takes place that evening. Thus the events on Cyprus appear to unfold within a day and a half.

Yet in this brief period the characters speak as if much more time were passing. Iago suggests that Desdemona has slept with

Cassio repeatedly in this time, while Bianca complains that Cassio has kept away from her for "seven days and nights." Emilia says Iago has "a hundred times / Woo'd me to steal" Desdemona's handkerchief, and Roderigo complains of having "wasted myself out of my means" since their arrival.

Why? Did Shakespeare compress events into a day and a half for his own convenience in plotting, relying on the hope that the timeline would "feel" longer to casual theatergoers? "I find it very hard to believe that he produced this impossible situation without knowing it," wrote A.C. Bradley in 1904. "It is one thing to read a drama or see it, quite another to construct and compose it, and he appears to have imagined the action in *Othello* with even more than his usual intensity."

• • •

BEATING THE NEWS

On Feb. 18, 1855, French-Canadian cattle dealer Louis Remme deposited $12,500 in gold in the Sacramento branch of the Adams & Company bank. Shortly afterward he received word that Page, Bacon & Company of St. Louis, the largest financial company west of the Alleghenies, had failed. He returned to the bank but it had already been liquidated, depleted by desperate depositors.

So Remme jumped on a horse and rode 665 miles north in 143 hours, including 10 hours of sleep and brief stops for food. He arrived in Portland, Ore., on Feb. 26, went straight to the Adams & Company bank, presented his certificate of deposit, and withdrew the $12,500. He had beaten the steamer that carried news of the bank's failure—and Portland had no telegraph.

• • •

LIMERICK

There was a young man of St. Bees
Who was stung in the arm by a wasp.
When they asked, "Does it hurt?"
He replied, "No, it doesn't;
I'm so glad it wasn't a hornet."

— W.S. Gilbert

• • •

FITTING

In the Dewey decimal system, books on number theory are labeled 512.81.
$512 = 2^9$ and $81 = 9^2$.

• • •

THE DIVESTITURE PUZZLE

Suppose you own stock in a company that you believe has acted immorally. You want to sell the stock, but is this morally permissible? If owning the stock is wrong, then selling it to another person amounts to abetting an immoral act. The buyer might not feel the stock is tainted, but you do.

Even just renouncing ownership amounts to redistributing

the stock's value among the other stockholders, which increases their moral culpability. CUNY philosopher Steven M. Cahn writes, "How then is principled divestiture possible?"

• • •

RIMSHOT

Two communists are sitting on the porch of a nudist colony.

One says, "Have you read Marx?"

The other says, "Yes, I think it's these wicker chairs."

(Dr. Johnson abominated puns. When Boswell suggested that perhaps he couldn't make them himself, Johnson said, "If I were punishéd for every pun I shed, there would not be left a puny shed for my punnish head.")

• • •

FOUND POETRY

William Whewell was a giant of 19th-century science, but he may have missed his true calling. Someone pointed out that his classic *Elementary Treatise on Mechanics* (1819) contains the following poetic sentence:

 And hence no force, however great,
can stretch a cord, however fine,
into a horizontal line
that shall be absolutely straight.

Then again, maybe not: Whewell quietly changed the wording in the next edition.

Max Beerbohm noticed a similar happenstance in the first edition of his collected works:

"London: John Lane, The Bodley Head
New York: Charles Scribner's Sons."
This plain announcement, nicely read,
Iambically runs.

• • •

BLOCKED

You have *n* cubical building blocks. You try to arrange them into
the largest possible solid cube, but you find that you don't have
quite enough blocks: One side of the large cube has exactly one
row too few.

Prove that *n* is divisible by 6.

(See Answers and Solutions)

• • •

A FOR EFFORT

Prospector William Schmidt was overjoyed when he struck gold
on California's Copper Mountain, but he faced one problem:
He was on the north side of the mountain, and the road to the
smelter was on the south side.

So he dug a tunnel.

He started in 1906, at age 35, working with a pick, a 4-pound
hammer, a hand drill, and dynamite. When he finally broke into
daylight on the mountain's south side, it was 1938 and he was 66
years old. He had single-handedly dug a tunnel 1,872 feet long,
displacing 2,600 cubic yards of granite.

Alas, success had to be its own reward. While Schmidt had
been digging, rail and road links had been built around the
mountain—so the tunnel was unnecessary.

• • •

THE GIRT DOG OF ENNERDALE

In 1810, a mysterious creature began killing sheep in northern England. Between May and September it defied the entire county of Cumberland, killing up to eight sheep a night despite being hunted nearly continuously. The "girt dog" never attacked the same flock on successive nights; it ignored poisoned meat left for it and led frustrated farmers on fruitless chases of 20 miles and more, occasionally turning to savage the forelegs of the pursuing dogs but never uttering a sound.

Finally, in September, the creature was run to ground near the Ehen River and shot. In four months it had killed more than 300 sheep. The carcass, which weighed 112 pounds, was stuffed and set up in a museum in Keswick, though it's since been lost. Its description—a tawny dog with a tiger's stripes—curiously matches that of the thylacine (above), a wolflike marsupial native to Tasmania. Possibly an exotic predator had escaped from a traveling menagerie and found itself peculiarly adapted to Cumberland farmland. We'll never know.

• • •

PREPARED

A young woman once asked Robert Peary, "But how does anyone know when he has reached the North Pole?"

"Nothing easier," Peary said. "One step beyond the pole, you see, and the north wind becomes a south one."

• • •

THE PULL OF FOUR

Think of any number and write it out in words. Count the number of letters and write that out in words. And so on:

- •SEVENTY-SEVEN (12 letters)
- •TWELVE (six letters)
- •SIX (three letters)
- •THREE (five letters)
- •FIVE (four letters)
- •FOUR (four letters)

If your spelling is good, you'll always arrive at FOUR.

• • •

A MARKETING PROBLEM

In 1938, poet Chard Powers Smith took a half-finished novel to Scribner's. They liked the text but objected to the title, which they thought would discourage customers. Smith agreed to change it, and the next year *The Artillery of Time* was published.

Smith's original title was *The Grapes of Wrath.*

Steinbeck's novel appeared a few weeks later.

• • •

THE WOW! SIGNAL

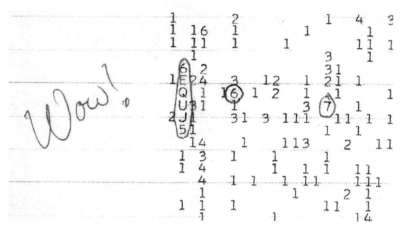

On Aug. 15, 1977, a telescope at Ohio State University detected a strong narrowband radio signal in the constellation Sagittarius—one so unusual that astronomer Jerry Ehman marked the printout with an exclamation.

The signal's intensity rose and then fell as the beam swept past its position in the sky. That's consistent with an extraterrestrial origin . . .but in 30 years and more than 100 searches, no one has been able to relocate it.

Without a recurrence, there's no way to know what Ehman's telescope heard that night—it's just a frustrating splash in a large, silent sea.

• • •

INKSMANSHIP

In 1863, the register of the U.S. Treasury, L.E. Chittenden, had to sign 12,500 bonds in a single weekend to stop the delivery of two British-built warships to the Confederacy. He started at noon on Friday and managed 3,700 signatures in the first seven hours, but by Saturday morning he was desperate:

 [E]very muscle on the right side connected with the movement of the hand and arm became inflamed, and the pain was almost beyond endurance. . . .In the slight pauses which were made, rubbing, the application of hot water, and other remedies were resorted to, in order to alleviate the pain and reduce the inflammation. They were comparatively ineffectual, and the hours dragged on without bringing much relief.

He finished, exhausted, at noon on Sunday, completing a mountain of bonds more than 6 feet high. These were rushed to a waiting steamer—and only then did word come that the English warships had been sold to a different buyer. The bonds, in the end, were not needed.

• • •

ROCK AND ROLL

Worshipful natives are rolling a giant statue of me across their island. The statue rests on a slab, which rests on rollers that have a circumference of 1 meter each. How far forward will the slab have moved when the rollers have made 1 revolution?

(See Answers and Solutions)

• • •

THE VOTING PARADOX

Suppose we hold an election with three candidates, X, Y, and Z. And suppose the voters fall into three groups:

Group 1 prefers, in order, X, Y, Z
Group 2 prefers, in order, Y, Z, X
Group 3 prefers, in order, Z, X, Y

Now, if Candidate X wins, his opponents can rightly object that a majority of voters would have preferred Candidate Z. And corresponding arguments can be made against the other candidates. So even though we've held a fair election, it's impossible to establish majority rule.

The Marquis de Condorcet noted this oddity in the 1700s; it's sometimes known as Condorcet's paradox.

• • •

OUTDONE

"It is not impossible that in a real dream of sleep, some one may have created an antagonist who beat him in an argument to prove that he was awake."

— Augustus De Morgan, *Formal Logic*, 1847

• • •

STEADY ON

Australia's Westfield ultramarathon had a surprise entrant in 1983: A 61-year-old potato farmer named Cliff Young arrived wearing overalls and gumboots and took a place among a field of 150 elite 20-somethings for the 543-mile run from Sydney to Melbourne.

Young ran with a peculiar shuffling gait that soon left him far behind the leaders, but as the race wore on he regained the ground rapidly. His strategy was simple: He didn't sleep. He had routinely rounded up sheep on his family's 2,000-acre ranch in Victoria, where he often ran two or three days without rest, and this preternatural endurance carried him easily into first place in the Westfield race, beating the record time by nearly two days.

At the finish Young said he'd been unaware there was a $10,000 prize; he gave it away to five other runners and returned quietly to his ranch. Asked what advice he'd give to other elderly runners, he said, "No matter what you do, you have to keep moving. If you don't wear out, you rust out."

• • •

THE HUMAN PAPERWEIGHT

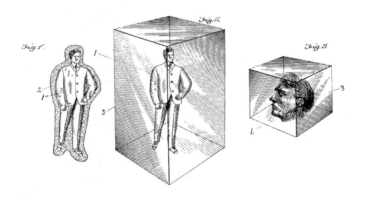

Thanks to Joseph Karwowski, you'll never have to say goodbye to your Uncle Julius. Patented in 1903, Karwowski's "method of preserving the dead" hermetically encases the corpse in a block of transparent glass to prevent decay and maintain a lifelike appearance.

Bonus: "In Fig. 3 I have shown the head only of the corpse as incased within the transparent block of glass, it being at once evident that the head alone may be preserved in this manner, if preferred."

• • •

THE MULTIPLIER

A 1784 letter from Ben Franklin to Benjamin Webb, an American in France who had applied for his aid:

 Dear Sir,

> I received yours of the 15th Instant, and the Memorial it inclosed. The account they give of your situation grieves me. I send you herewith a Bill for Ten Louis d'ors. I do not pretend to *give* such a Sum; I only *lend* it to you. When you shall return to your Country with a good Character, you cannot fail of getting into some Business, that will in time enable you to pay all your Debts. In that Case, when you meet with another honest Man in similar Distress, you must pay me by lending this Sum to him; enjoining him to discharge the Debt by a like operation, when he shall be able, and shall meet with another opportunity. I hope it may thus go thro' many hands, before it meets with a Knave that will stop its Progress. This is a trick of mine for doing a deal of good with a little money. I am not rich enough to afford *much* in good works, and so am obliged to be cunning and make the most of a *little*. With best wishes for the success of your Memorial, and your future prosperity, I am, dear Sir, your most obedient servant,
>
> B. Franklin.

• • •

FIRST CLASS

When Canada Post routes letters to Santa Claus, it uses the postal code "H0H 0H0".

•••

LIGHT WORK

From Lewis Carroll:

 I don't know if you are fond of puzzles, or not. If you are, try this. . . .A gentleman (a nobleman let us say, to make it more interesting) had a sitting-room with only one window in it—a square window, 3 feet high and 3 feet wide. Now he had weak eyes, and the window gave too much light, *so* (don't you like '*so*' in a story?) he sent for the builder, and told him to alter it, so as only to give half the light. Only, he was to keep it square—he was to keep it 3 feet high—and he was to keep it 3 feet wide. How did he do it? Remember, he wasn't allowed to use curtains, or shutters, or coloured glass, or anything of that sort.

(See Answers and Solutions)

•••

CHARGED WORDS

On the night of Sept. 2, 1859, an enormous solar flare produced brilliant auroras around the world. Newspapers and ships' logs reported striking displays throughout the United States, Europe, Japan, and Australia; Bostonians could read by their light at 1 a.m.

At the height of the storm, a curious conversation took place between two New England telegraph operators:

 Boston: Please cut off your battery, and let us see if we cannot work with the auroral current alone.

Portland, Maine: I have done so. Will you do the same?

Boston: I have cut my battery off and connected the line with the earth. We are working with the current from the Aurora Borealis alone. How do you receive my writing?

Portland: Very well indeed. Much better than with the batteries on. There is much less variation in the current, and the magnets work steadier. Suppose we continue to work so until the Aurora subsides?

Boston: Agreed. Are you ready for business?

Portland: Yes; go ahead.

They carried on in this way for two hours, the storm inducing enough current in the lines to support their transmissions. It marked the first conclusive link between auroral activity and electricity.

● ● ●

THE SOMERTON MAN

On Dec. 1, 1948, a bather discovered a body on the beach near Adelaide, Australia. The man appeared to be European, about 45 years old, well dressed, and in excellent physical condition. Indeed, the coroner could not determine a cause of death. Still more strangely, it seemed the man had carried no money, and all identifying marks had been removed from his clothes. Apparently he had left a suitcase at the Adelaide railway station, but it contained no useful clues. Photos and fingerprints were circulated throughout the English-speaking world, but no one identified him.

And the body bore one last strange clue: In a trouser fob

pocket, one of the investigators found a tiny piece of paper bearing the words "Taman Shud." Those are the final words in the *Rubaiyat of Omar Khayyam*; they mean "The End." A local doctor came forward with a copy of that book, from which the words had been clipped. He had found it tossed on the front seat of his car the day before the body was found.

But even that clue went nowhere. To this day, no one knows who the man was or how he died. He's known only as the Somerton man.

• • •

GIFTED

" 'Did you hear the story of the extraordinary precocity of Mrs. Perkins's baby that died last week?' asked Mrs. Allgood. 'It was only three months old, and lying at the point of death, when the grief-stricken mother asked the doctor if nothing could save it. "Absolutely nothing!" said the doctor. Then the infant looked up pitifully into its mother's face and said—absolutely nothing!'

'Impossible!' insisted Mildred. 'And only three months old!'

— Henry Ernest Dudeney, *Amusements in Mathematics*, 1917

• • •

UNQUOTE

"I have often wondered how it is that every man loves himself more than all the rest of men, but yet sets less value on his own opinion of himself than on the opinion of others."

—Marcus Aurelius

• • •

ERDÖS NUMBERS

Hungarian mathematician Paul Erdös was immensely prolific—he published about 1,500 articles in his lifetime. His influence is so great that his colleagues have taken to assigning "Erdös numbers" to one another. Erdös himself gets an Erdös number of 0; his direct collaborators get a 1; anyone who collaborates with them gets a 2, and so on.

Those in the first rank include many of the world's top mathematicians, but there's one standout: Hank Aaron. The Baseball Hall of Famer once signed a baseball with Erdös while accepting an honorary degree—and that, some say, counts as a joint publication.

• • •

E-LIMINATED

Gadsby is a 50,000-word novel that doesn't use the letter E:

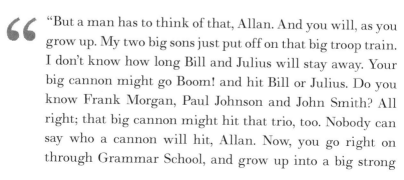

"But a man has to think of that, Allan. And you will, as you grow up. My two big sons just put off on that big troop train. I don't know how long Bill and Julius will stay away. Your big cannon might go Boom! and hit Bill or Julius. Do you know Frank Morgan, Paul Johnson and John Smith? All right; that big cannon might hit that trio, too. Nobody can say who a cannon will hit, Allan. Now, you go right on through Grammar School, and grow up into a big strong man, and don't think about war;" and Gadsby, standing and gazing far off to Branton Hills' charming hill district, thought: "I think that will bust up a wild young ambition!"

The author, Ernest Vincent Wright, notes that he could mention no numbers between 6 and 30. And "When introducing young ladies into the story, this is a real barrier; for what young woman wants to have it known that she is over thirty?"

• • •

RELATIVE LOGIC

You say that you have a dog.

Yes, and a villain of a one, said Ctesippus.

And he has puppies?

Yes, and they are very like himself.

And the dog is the father of them?

Yes, he said, I certainly saw him and the mother of the puppies come together.

And is he not yours?

To be sure he is.

Then he is a father, and he is yours; ergo he is your father, and the puppies are your brothers.

Let me ask you one little question more, said Dionysodorus, quickly interposing, in order that Ctesippus might not get in his word: You beat this dog?

Ctesippus said, laughing: Indeed I do; and I only wish that I could beat you instead of him.

Then you beat your father, he said.

— Plato, *Euthydemus*

• • •

THE NECKTIE PARADOX

You and I are having an argument. Our wives have given us new neckties, and we're arguing over which is more expensive.

Finally we agree to a wager. We'll ask our wives for the prices, and whoever is wearing the more expensive tie has to give it to the other.

You think, "The odds are in my favor. If I lose the wager, I lose only the value of my tie. If I win the wager, I gain more than the value of my tie. On balance I come out ahead."

The trouble is, I'm thinking the same thing. Are we both right?

• • •

TRAFFIC FORECAST

John Macnie's 1883 utopian novel *The Diothas* describes paved roads on which cars achieve speeds of 20 miles per hour:

 When we had fairly emerged into the country, the curricle, gradually increasing its speed, moved over the smooth track like a shadow, obedient to the slightest touch of its guide. Steering was effected much as in the tricycle of the present: the brakes were controlled by the feet. The forefinger, by means of a lever resembling the brake of a bicycle, regulated the amount of force allowed to issue from the reservoir.

That's not the remarkable part, though. "'You see the white line running along the centre of the road,' resumed Utis. 'The rule of the road requires that line to be kept on the left except when passing a vehicle in front. Then the line may be crossed, provided the way on that side is clear.'"

• • •

RHYMING THE UNRHYMABLE

I have tried a hundred times, I guess,
To find a rhyme for month;
I have failed a hundred times, I know,
But succeeded the hundred and one-th.

There were two men a training went.
It was in December month;
One had his bayonet thrown away,
The other had his gun th-
rown away.

— *Miscellaneous Notes and Queries*, August 1894

• • •

THE FLANNAN ISLES MYSTERY

On Dec. 15, 1900, a passing steamer noticed that the lighthouse on Scotland's Flannan Isles had gone dark. A relief crew, arriving on Dec. 26, found that the flagstaff was bare, the beds were unmade, the clock was stopped . . .and there was no trace of the three men who manned the lighthouse.

A chair had been overturned by the kitchen table, but otherwise there were no signs of disturbance. The lamps had been cleaned and refilled, the entrance gate and main door had been closed, and a set of oilskins were found inside, which was strange, considering the violent weather.

As they explored further, the relief crew discovered at the island's west landing signs of damage that were "difficult to believe unless actually seen." An iron railway was wrenched out of its concrete, a rock weighing more than a ton had been displaced, and turf had been ripped from a clifftop 200 feet above sea level. But the keepers had kept their log after this point.

What really happened? An investigation suggested that the three were swept away while trying to secure a box on the west landing. But no one really knows.

• • •

HOLD THE MILK

The Arecibo Observatory is the largest single-aperture telescope ever built.

Astronomer Frank Drake calculated the dish would hold 357 million boxes of corn flakes.

• • •

WALKING ON AIR

"Space isn't remote at all. It's only an hour's drive away if your car could go straight upwards." —Astronomer Fred Hoyle

• • •

IN A WORD

macropicide
n. a slayer of kangaroos

drollic
adj. of or pertaining to puppet shows

callipygian
adj. having beautiful buttocks

speustic
adj. baked in haste

• • •

BREAKING BAD

Amy and Betty are playing a game. They have a chocolate bar that's 8 squares long and 6 squares wide. Amy begins by breaking the bar in two along any division. Betty can then pick up any piece and break it in two, and so on. The first player who cannot move will be clapped in chains and rocketed off to a lifetime of soul-destroying toil in the cobalt mines of Yongar Zeta. (I know, it's a pretty brutal game.) Who will win?

(See Answers and Solutions)

• • •

"CALCULATING GIRL"

“ In the spring of 1819, a little girl, about eleven years old, appeared at the Royal Exchange, and made some very extraordinary calculations. Several gentlemen asked her some intricate question, and while they were calculating it, she gave a correct answer. She was asked to multiply 525,600 by 250; which she answered in one minute, 131,400,000. A second question was, how many minutes there are in forty-two years? Answer, 22,075,200. She was next desired to multiply 525,000 by 450; answer, 236,250,000. Several other questions, equally difficult, were put, all of which she answered very correctly. It is remarkable, that the girl could neither read nor write. She stated herself to be the daughter of a weaver, living at Mile-End, New Town, of the name of Heywood.

— *Cabinet of Curiosities, Natural, Artificial,*
and Historical, 1822

• • •

FIRST THINGS FIRST

In 1963, Giants pitcher Gaylord Perry joked, "They'll put a man on the moon before I hit a home run."

On July 20, 1969, just minutes after Apollo 11 made its lunar landing, he hit the first home run of his career.

• • •

THE ELEVATOR PARADOX

In the 1950s, physicists George Gamow and Moritz Stern worked in the same seven-story building. Gamow, on the second floor, noticed that the first elevator to arrive at his office was most often going down. For Stern, on the sixth floor, the first elevator was most often going up. It was as if elves were manufacturing elevator cars in the middle of the building.

You can observe the same phenomenon in most tall buildings, and there are no elves involved. Do you see why it occurs?

• • •

WELL, HEY!

 How to Cure Cancer.—Boil down the inner bark of red and white oak to the consistency of molasses; apply as a plaster, shifting it once a week; or, burn red-oak bark to ashes; sprinkle it on the sore till it is eaten out; then apply a plaster of tar; or, take garget berries and leaves of stramonium; simmer them together in equal parts of neatsfoot oil and the tops of hemlock; mix well together, and apply it to the parts affected; at the same time make a tea of winter-green (root and branch); put a handful into two quarts of water; add two ounces of sulphur and drink of this tea freely during the day.

— *Barkham Burroughs' Encyclopaedia of Astounding Facts and Useful Information*, 1889

• • •

CELESTIAL

Each book in Dante's *Divine Comedy* ends with the word *stars*.

PART SEVEN

PASSPORTS, CORNED BEEF, *and* THE MONA LISA

THE CLEVE CARTMILL AFFAIR

In 1943, writer Cleve Cartmill proposed a story about a futuristic bomb to John W. Campbell, the editor of *Astounding Science Fiction*. Campbell liked the idea and gave him some background material on fission devices and uranium-235.

The story, "Deadline," ran in Campbell's March 1944 issue—and shortly brought a visit from the FBI. Apparently the technical details in Cartmill's story had some uncomfortable resonances with the top-secret Manhattan Project, then under way at Los Alamos:

 Two cast-iron hemispheres, clamped over the orange segments of cadmium alloy. And the fuse—I see it is in—a tiny can of cadmium in a beryllium holder and a small explosive powerful enough to shatter the cadmium walls. Then—correct me if I'm wrong, will you?—the powdered uranium oxide runs together in the central cavity. The radium shoots neutrons into this mass—and the U-235 takes over from there. Right?

Campbell explained that he'd studied atomic physics at MIT and had drawn the research from unclassified journals. In the end the authorities were satisfied—but they asked him not to publish any more stories on nuclear technology.

• • •

TREVANION'S ESCAPE

Confined in Colchester Castle during the English civil war, the royalist officer Sir John Trevanion was awaiting execution when he received this letter:

 Worthie Sir John:- Hope, that is ye beste comfort of ye afflicted, cannot much, I fear me, help you now. That I would saye to you, is this only: if ever I may be able to requite that I do owe you, stand not upon asking me. 'Tis not much that I can do: but what I can do, bee ye verie sure I wille. I knowe that, if dethe comes, if ordinary men fear it, it frights not you, accounting it for a high honor, to have such a rewarde of your loyalty. Pray yet that you may be spared this soe bitter, cup. I fear not that you will grudge any sufferings; only if bie submission you can turn them away, 'tis the part of a wise man. Tell me, an if you can, to do for you anythinge that you wolde have done. The general goes back on Wednesday. Restinge your servant to command.—R.T.

Sir John studied the message for several hours, and then, apparently despairing, asked to spend some time alone in prayer. His captors agreed—and never saw him again.

Read the third letter after each punctuation mark.

• • •

HOMEWORK

It's been known since 1876 that $2^{67}-1$ isn't prime, but for decades no one knew what the factors were.

Then, at a meeting in 1903, mathematician Frank Nelson

Cole gave an hourlong "lecture" in which he didn't say a word. On one chalkboard he expanded the value of $2^{67}-1$:

147,573,952,589,676,412,927

On another he wrote:

193,707,721 × 761,838,257,287

Then he multiplied those values by hand. The two boards matched. He had found the factors. Cole returned to his seat amid a standing ovation.

He later admitted that finding the factors had taken "three years of Sundays."

$$\bullet \; \bullet \; \bullet$$

COMPLAINT

A letter to the London *Times*, Feb. 17, 1915:

 Sir,

> A little light might be shed, with advantage, upon the high-handed methods of the Passport Department at the Foreign Office. On the form provided for the purpose, I described my face as 'intelligent'. Instead of finding this characterization entered, I have received a passport on which some official utterly unknown to me has taken it upon himself to call my face 'oval'.

> Yours very truly,
> Bassett Digby

• • •

CONTRABAND

Astronaut John Young smuggled a corned beef sandwich into space. As Gemini 3 was circling Earth in March 1965, Young pulled the sandwich out of his pocket and offered it to Gus Grissom:

Grissom: What is it?

Young: Corned beef sandwich.

Grissom: Where did that come from?

Young: I brought it with me. Let's see how it tastes. Smells, doesn't it?

Grissom: Yes, it's breaking up. I'm going to stick it in my pocket.

Young: Is it? It was a thought, anyway.

"Wally Schirra had the sandwich made up at a restaurant at Cocoa Beach a couple of days before, and I hid it in a pocket of my space suit," Young explained later. "Gus had been bored by the official menus we'd practiced with in training, and it seemed like a fun idea at the time."

Grissom wrote, "After the flight our superiors at NASA let us know in no uncertain terms that non-man-rated corned beef sandwiches were out for future space missions. But John's deadpan offer of this strictly non-regulation goodie remains one of the highlights of our flight for me."

• • •

THE TWO-ENVELOPE PARADOX

Here are two envelopes. One contains twice as much money as the other. You must choose one, and then consider whether to keep it or exchange it for mine. Which should you do?

It would seem advantageous to switch: Depending on which envelope you started with, you'll either lose a little or gain a lot. If your unopened envelope contains $10, for example, the other must contain $5 or $20.

So we trade envelopes and I offer you the same deal. But now the same reasoning applies, so it makes sense to trade again. Indeed, it seems reasonable to keep exchanging envelopes forever, without ever opening one. How can this be?

• • •

INTERLUDE

A little girl asked George Ade, "Does M-I-R-A-G-E spell marriage?"

He said, "Yes."

• • •

TWO REVOLUTIONARIES

The key to the Bastille resides at Mount Vernon.

The Marquis de Lafayette had served under George Washington during the American Revolution, and when the French political prison fell in 1790 he sent the key to his former commander.

"Give me leave, my dear General," he wrote, "to present you with a picture of the Bastille, just as it looked a few days after I had ordered its demolition,—with the main key of the fortress of despotism. It is a tribute, which I owe, as a son to my adoptive father, as an Aide-de-Camp to my General, as a Missionary of liberty to its Patriarch."

• • •

THE TWO CULTURES

Tennyson's poem "The Vision of Sin" contains this couplet:

> Every moment dies a man,
> Every moment one is born.

When he published it in 1842, Charles Babbage sent him a note:

> I need hardly point out to you that this calculation would tend to keep the sum total of the world's population in a state of perpetual equipoise, whereas it is a well-known fact that the said sum total is constantly on the increase. I would therefore take the liberty of suggesting that, in the next edition of your excellent poem, the erroneous calculation to which I refer should be corrected as follows:—

Every moment dies a man,
And one and a sixteenth is born.

"I may add that the exact figures are 1.167," he added, "but something must, of course, be conceded to the laws of metre."

• • •

UNDERPAID

   Early one morning [George III] met a boy in the stables at Windsor and said: 'Well, boy! What do you do? What do they pay you?'

   'I help in the stable,' said the boy, 'but they only give me victuals and clothes.'

   'Be content,' said George, 'I have no more.'

— Beckles Willson, *George III*, 1907

• • •

FUTURE TENSE

When he wasn't inventing logarithms, John Napier took a keen interest in military affairs. In 1596 he composed a list of war machines that "by the grace of God and worke of expert craftsmen" he hoped to produce "for defence of this Iland." These included a piece of artillery that could "clear a field of four miles circumference of all living creatures exceeding a foot of height," a chariot like "a moving mouth of mettle" that would "scatter destruction on all sides," and "devises of sayling under water, with divers and other strategems for harming of the enemyes."

No one knows whether Napier built his machines, but by

World War I they were certainly realities—he had foreseen the machine gun, the tank, and the submarine.

• • •

"DUST COVER FOR DOG"

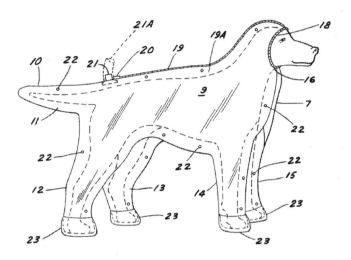

Well, maybe you'll need one someday.

Seroun Kesh's 1964 invention has a bonus application: You can attach a hair dryer to tube 21 "so that the same may be used to dry the dog after a bath."

• • •

ART HISTORY

In 1989, a Philadelphia financial analyst visited a flea market in Adamstown, Pa., spotted an old painting whose frame he liked, and purchased it for $4.

When he removed the frame, he found a folded document between the picture canvas and the wood backing. And the document appeared to be the Declaration of Independence.

It was. He had discovered an original copy of the Declaration, from its first printing in 1776. Sotheby's auctioned it for $2.42 million in 1991, then again for $8.14 million in 2000.

"This was how Congress voted to disseminate the news of independence," said Sotheby's vice chairman, David Redden. "So it was printed up from Thomas Jefferson's draft of the Declaration and then sent around by couriers to the armies in the field, to the newly independent colonies, to the committees of public safety, and surely to the British, too."

How it had got into the painting is unknown.

• • •

"THE TEN TRAVELERS"

Ten weary, footsore travelers,
All in a woeful plight,
Sought shelter at a wayside inn
One dark and stormy night.

"Nine beds—no more," the landlord said,
"Have I to offer you;
To each of eight a single room,
But the ninth must serve for two."

A din arose. The troubled host
Could only scratch his head,
For of those tired men, not two
Could occupy one bed.

The puzzled host was soon at ease —
He was a clever man —
And so to please his guests devised
This most ingenious plan.

In room marked A, two men were placed,
The third he lodged in B,
The fourth to C was then assigned —
The fifth retired to D.

In E the sixth he tucked away,
In F the seventh man;
The eighth and ninth in G and H,
And then to A he ran,

Wherein the host, as I have said,
Had laid two travelers by;
Then taking one, the tenth and last,
He lodged him safe in I.

Nine single rooms—a room for each —
Were made to serve for ten.
And this it is that puzzles me
And many wiser men.

— S.R. Ford, *Ford's Christian Repository
& Home Circle*, May 1888

• • •

PEN PALS

"Guess whose birthday it is today?" Franklin Pierce Adams
asked Beatrice Kaufman.

"Yours?" she guessed.

"No, but you're getting warm," he said. "It's Shakespeare's!"

• • •

FAIR EXCHANGE

An admirer once wrote to Rudyard Kipling: "I see you get a dollar a word for your writing. I enclose a check for one dollar. Please send me a sample."

Kipling responded: "Thanks."

• • •

SFORZANDO

What do you get when you drop a piano down a mineshaft? A-flat minor.

•••

GUN CONTROL

" Only four days ago, right in the next farm house to the one where I am spending the summer, a grandmother, old and gray and sweet, one of the loveliest spirits in the land, was sitting at her work, when her young grandson crept in and got down an old, battered, rusty gun which had not been touched for many years and was supposed not to be loaded, and pointed it at her, laughing, and threatening to shoot. In her fright she ran screaming and pleading toward the door on the other side of the room; but as she passed him he placed the gun almost against her very breast and pulled the trigger! He had supposed it was not loaded. And he was right: it wasn't. So there wasn't any harm done.

— Mark Twain, "Advice to Youth," 1882

•••

THE POTATO PARADOX

You have 100 pounds of Martian potatoes, which are 99 percent water by weight. You let them dehydrate until they're 98 percent water. How much do they weigh now?

(See Answers and Solutions)

•••

UNQUOTE

"If one only wished to be happy, this could be easily accomplished; but we wish to be happier than other people, and this is always difficult, for we believe others to be happier than they are."

—Montesquieu

• • •

SMILE

In 1911, Argentine con man Eduardo de Valfierno found a way to steal the Mona Lisa six times over at no risk to himself.

First he made private deals with six separate buyers to steal and deliver the priceless painting. He hired a professional art restorer to make six fakes, and shipped them in advance to the buyers' locales (to avoid later trouble with customs).

Then he paid a thief to steal the original from the Louvre, and when news of the theft had spread he delivered the six fakes to their recipients, exacting a high price for each. Then he quietly disappeared. The flummoxed thief was soon caught trying to sell the red-hot original, and it was returned to the museum in 1913.

• • •

APROPOS

How many letters are in ACE KING QUEEN JACK TEN NINE
EIGHT SEVEN SIX FIVE FOUR THREE TWO?

Fifty-two.

(This also works in Spanish.)

• • •

SUSPENSE

At Oxford, Oscar Wilde was required to translate a passage from
the Greek version of the New Testament. Satisfied, the examiner
stopped him.

"Oh, do let me go on," said Wilde. "I want to see how it ends."

• • •

FORE!

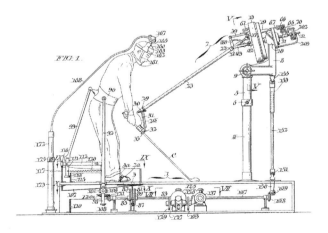

In 1949, George Jenks patented this apparatus "for ultimate at-
tainment of an ideal golf swing."

G.K. Chesterton wrote, "I regard golf as an expensive way of playing marbles."

• • •

DOUBLE DUTY

LIST and ROLL are synonyms in two different senses. Both mean to tilt—and both refer to a series of names.

• • •

GENDER ISSUES

In a certain kingdom, boys and girls are born in strictly equal proportions. Determined to increase the proportion of women in the land, the sultan issues a decree: Any woman who bears a son is forbidden to have any further children. He reasons that some families will thus contain multiple daughters but a single son.

A number of years pass, and the sultan is confused to find that the kingdom still contains an equal number of boys and girls. Why?

(See Answers and Solutions)

• • •

ERRATUM

It's important to acknowledge your mistakes. In a 1920 editorial, the *New York Times* attacked Robert Goddard's claim that a rocket would work in space:

> That Professor Goddard, with his 'chair' in Clark College and the countenancing of the Smithsonian Institution, does not know the relation of action to reaction, and of the need to have something better than a vacuum against which to react—to say that would be absurd. Of course he only seems to lack the knowledge ladled out daily in high schools.

In 1969, days before Apollo 11 landed on the moon, it published this correction:

> Further investigation and experimentation have confirmed the findings of Isaac Newton in the 17th century, and it is now definitely established that a rocket can function in a vacuum as well as in an atmosphere.

It added: "The *Times* regrets the error."

• • •

FIVE DOWN

In May 1944, as the Allies prepared to invade Europe, the word UTAH appeared in a crossword puzzle in Britain's *Daily Telegraph*. Security officers found that a bit worrisome: Utah was the code name for one of the landing beaches.

Their worry turned to alarm when OMAHA and MULBERRY, two further code names, appeared in subsequent puzzles. And alarm turned to panic when NEPTUNE and OVERLORD appeared four days before the planned invasion. In Allied code, Neptune referred to the landing operation, Overlord to the entire invasion of Normandy. The government immediately arrested Leonard Dawe, the schoolteacher who had composed the puzzles.

A long interrogation ensued, but in the end they decided Dawe was innocent. Apparently his students had overheard troops using these words and then repeated them in his hearing. If that's true, the published words were in fact code names—but no one involved had recognized them as such.

• • •

IN A WORD

acnestis
n. that part of an animal's skin that it cannot reach to scratch

qualtagh
n. the first person one meets after leaving the house

eyeservice
n. work done only while an employer is watching

jentacular
adj. pertaining to breakfast

• • •

THE PRISONERS' PARADOX

Three condemned prisoners share a cell. A guard arrives and tells them that one has been pardoned.

"Which is it?" they ask.

"I can't tell you that," says the guard. "I can't tell a prisoner his own fate."

Prisoner A takes the guard aside. "Look," he says. "Of the three of us, only one has been pardoned. That means that one of my cellmates is still sure to die. Give me his name. That way you're not telling me my own fate, and you're not identifying the pardoned man."

The guard thinks about this and tells him, "Prisoner B is sure to die."

Prisoner A rejoices that his own chance of survival has improved from 1/3 to 1/2. But how is this possible? The guard has given him no new information. Has he?

• • •

ACCIDENTALLY FAMOUS

In 1838, a man made history by having his boots polished.

The man, in the lower left, was the only thing standing still when Louis Daguerre took this photograph of a busy Parisian street. Because the film was exposed for 10 minutes, the rest of the traffic blurred into nothing—and the anonymous man became the first person ever to appear in a photograph.

• • •

EQUAL OPPORTUNITY

She frowned and called him Mr.
Because in sport he Kr.
And so in spite
That very night
This Mr. Kr. Sr.

— Anonymous

• • •

RICHARD'S PARADOX

Clearly there are integers so huge they can't be described in fewer than 22 syllables. Put them all in a big pile and consider the smallest one. It's "the smallest integer that can't be described in fewer than 22 syllables."

That phrase has 21 syllables.

• • •

UNQUOTE

"We don't know a millionth of one percent about anything."

—Thomas Edison

• • •

PERPETUAL LOCOMOTION

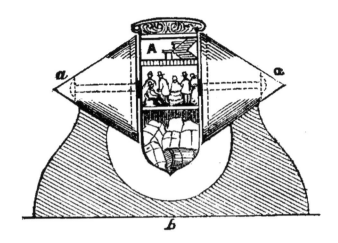

In 1829 a correspondent to the *Mechanic's Magazine* proposed this design for a "self-moving railway carriage." Fill the car with passengers and cargo as shown and set it on two rails that undulate across the landscape:

In the descending sections (*a*, *c*, *e*) the two rails are parallel. In the ascending ones (*b*, *d*) they diverge so that the car, mounted on cones, will roll forward to settle more deeply between them, paradoxically "ascending" the slope. If the track circles the world the car will "assuredly continue to roll along in one undeviating course until time shall be no more."

"How any one could ever imagine that such a contrivance would ever continue in motion for even a short time . . .must be a puzzle to every sane mechanic," wrote John Phin in *The Seven Follies of Science* in 1911. But what does he know?

• • •

WORKING LATE

 For twenty-five years past an oral addition to the written standing orders of the native guard at Government House, near Poona, had been communicated regularly from one guard to another, on relief, to the effect that any cat passing out of the front door after dark was to be regarded as His Excellency the Governor, and to be saluted accordingly. The meaning of this was that Sir Robert Grant, Governor of Bombay, had died there in 1838, and on the evening of the day of his death a cat was seen to leave the house by the front door and walk up and down a particular path, as had been the Governor's habit to do, after sunset. A Hindu sentry had observed this, and he mentioned it to others of his faith, who made it a subject of superstitious conjecture, the result being that one of the priestly class explained the mystery of the dogma of the transmigration of the soul from one body to another, and interpreted the circumstance to mean that the spirit of the deceased Governor had entered into one of the house pets. It was difficult to fix on a particular one, and it was therefore decided that every cat passing out of the main entrance after dark was to be regarded as the tabernacle of Governor Grant's soul, and to be treated with due respect and the proper honours. This decision was accepted without question by all the native attendants and others belonging to Government House. The whole guard, from sepoy to subadar, fully acquiesced in it, and an oral addition was made to the standing orders that the sentry at the front door would 'present arms' to any cat passing out there after dark.

— Sir Thomas Edward Gordon, *A Varied Life*, 1906

•••

BREAD ALONE

Andy and Bill are traveling when they meet Carl. Andy has 5 loaves of bread and Bill has 3; Carl has none and asks to share theirs, promising to pay them 8 gold pieces when they reach the next town.

They agree and divide the bread equally among them. When they reach the next town, Carl offers 5 gold pieces to Andy and 3 to Bill.

"Excuse me," says Andy. "That's not equitable." He proposes another arrangement, which, on consideration, Bill and Carl agree is correct and fair.

How do they divide the 8 gold pieces?

(See Answers and Solutions)

•••

NATURALLY

Someone once asked Jean Cocteau, "Suppose your house were on fire and you could remove only one thing. What would you take?"

Cocteau considered, then said, "I would take the fire."

•••

UNCONDITIONAL

When the 18-year-old Ethel Barrymore informed her father that she was engaged, he wired:

CONGRATULATIONS LOVE FATHER

When she informed him she'd broken it off, he wrote:

CONGRATULATIONS LOVE FATHER

• • •

INSIDE STRAIGHT

Draw any two lines, pick three points on each, and lace them all together like so:

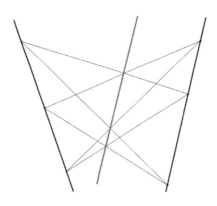

The crossings of the laces will always form a straight line.

• • •

DUELING DOPPELGÄNGERS

When World War I broke out in August 1914, Germany enlisted a large ocean liner, the *Cap Trafalgar*, to attack British merchant ships around Cape Horn. While at a supply base on Trinidade,

it was surprised by the HMS *Carmania*, a British liner that had
been similarly pressed into service by the British navy.

The two enormous ships squared off and fought a murderous
sea battle. In the end the *Cap Trafalgar* sank, and the *Carmania*
limped away to a Brazilian port.

An observer might still have wondered which side won—by
an ironic coincidence, the *Cap Trafalgar* had been disguised as
the *Carmania* and the *Carmania* as the *Cap Trafalgar*.

• • •

HOPE AND CHANGE

Three men stop at a hotel and agree to share a room for $30.
Each gives the desk clerk $10.

Later, the clerk realizes he's overcharged them for the room
by $5. He gives the bellboy five $1 bills and tells him to return
the money to the three men. The unscrupulous bellboy keeps $2
for himself and gives $1 to each of the three men.

So the men paid $9 each for the room, for a total of $27. The
bellboy has $2. What happened to the other dollar?

(See Answers and Solutions)

• • •

PHILOSOPHY

66 One day there was a traveller in the woods in California,
in the dry season, when the Trades were blowing strong.
He had ridden a long way, and he was tired and hungry,
and dismounted from his horse to smoke a pipe. But when

he felt in his pocket he found but two matches. He struck the first, and it would not light.

'Here is a pretty state of things!' said the traveller. 'Dying for a smoke; only one match left; and that certain to miss fire! Was there ever a creature so unfortunate? And yet,' thought the traveller, 'suppose I light this match, and smoke my pipe, and shake out the dottle here in the grass — the grass might catch on fire, for it is dry like tinder; and while I snatch out the flames in front, they might evade and run behind me, and seize upon yon bush of poison oak; before I could reach it, that would have blazed up; over the bush I see a pine tree hung with moss; that too would fly in fire upon the instant to its topmost bough; and the flame of that long torch—how would the trade wind take and brandish that through the inflammable forest! I hear this dell roar in a moment with the joint voice of wind and fire, I see myself gallop for my soul, and the flying conflagration chase and outflank me through the hills; I see this pleasant forest burn for days, and the cattle roasted, and the springs dried up, and the farmer ruined, and his children cast upon the world. What a world hangs upon this moment!'

With that he struck the match, and it missed fire.

'Thank God!' said the traveller, and put his pipe in his pocket.

— Robert Louis Stevenson, "Fables,"
Longman's Magazine, August 1895

• • •

AN UNREADABLE BOOK

Some writers seem to crave anonymity. None more so than the
author of the Voynich manuscript, who invented a mysterious
language and an unknown alphabet that has been defying schol-
ars for 500 years.

To judge from the illustrations, the text deals with astronomy,
biology, cosmology, herbs, and recipes. Handwriting experts say
that the glyphs were written with speed and care, as if the author
were facile with them. Statistical analysis seems to show that it's
a natural language, but the vocabulary is unusually small, and
in some ways it seems to resemble Arabic more than European
languages.

Because no one knows precisely what the 240-page book is, it's hard to guess who wrote it. Suspects include a who's who of Europe in the Middle Ages, Roger Bacon and John Dee among them. The cipher has resisted even the National Security Agency, leading some to think it's a hoax, but even that is hard to prove conclusively.

There's a great irony at the bottom of this. The mysterious author was one of the most successful cryptographers in history—so successful, in fact, that we may never know who he was.

PART EIGHT

SQUIRRELS, THE MAYFLOWER,
and THE DECLARATION OF
INDEPENDENCE

ARGUING IN CIRCLES

66 Some years ago, being with a camping party in the mountains, I returned from a solitary ramble to find every one
engaged in a ferocious metaphysical dispute. The corpus
of the dispute was a squirrel—a live squirrel supposed to
be clinging to one side of a tree-trunk; while over against
the tree's opposite side a human being was imagined to
stand. This human witness tries to get sight of the squirrel
by moving rapidly round the tree, but no matter how fast
he goes, the squirrel moves as fast in the opposite direction, and always keeps the tree between himself and the
man, so that never a glimpse of him is caught. The resul-
tant metaphysical problem now is this: *Does the man go
round the squirrel or not?*

— William James, *Pragmatism*, 1907

• • •

YABLO'S PARADOX

All the statements below this one are false.
All the statements below this one are false.
All the statements below this one are false.
All the statements below this one are false.
All the statements below this one are false.
...

These statements can't all be false, because that would make the first one true, a contradiction. But neither can any one of them be true, as a true statement would have to be followed by an infinity of false statements, and the falsity of any one of them implies the truth of some that follow. Thus there's no consistent way to assign truth values to all the statements.

This is reminiscent of the well-known liar paradox ("This sentence is false"), except that none of the sentences above refers to itself. MIT philosopher Stephen Yablo uses it to show that circularity is not necessary to produce a paradox.

• • •

THE SILENT CITY

In 1885, explorer Richard Willoughby claimed to have discovered a wonderful mirage above Alaska's Muir glacier: He'd seen a modern city, he said, with buildings, church towers, vessels, even citizens. This photograph sold "like hot cakes" in the summer of 1889, and Willoughby sold the negative to a San Francisco photographer for $500.

There it all unraveled. An American consul, home from England, noted that the "silent city" bore a striking resemblance to Bristol. It turned out that Willoughby had paid an English tourist $10 for an overexposed photo of his hometown, and the rest was hot air. Still, he deserves credit for invention.

• • •

SELF SEEKING

Letter from Winston Churchill to American author Winston Churchill, June 1899:

 Mr. Winston Churchill presents his compliments to Mr. Winston Churchill, and begs to draw his attention to a matter which concerns them both. He has learnt from the Press notices that Mr. Winston Churchill proposes to bring out another novel, entitled *Richard Carvel*, which is certain to have a considerable sale both in England and America. Mr. Winston Churchill is also the author of a novel now being published in serial form in *Macmillan's Magazine*, and for which he anticipates some sale both in England and America. He also proposes to publish on the 1st of October another military chronicle on the Soudan War. He has no doubt that Mr. Winston Churchill will recognise from this letter—if indeed by no other means— that there is grave danger of his works being mistaken for those of Mr. Winston Churchill. He feels sure that Mr. Winston Churchill desires this as little as he does himself. In future to avoid mistakes as far as possible, Mr. Winston Churchill has decided to sign all published articles, stories, or other works, 'Winston Spencer Churchill,' and not 'Winston Churchill' as formerly. He trusts that this arrangement will commend itself to Mr. Winston Churchill, and he ventures to suggest, with a view to preventing further confusion which may arise out of this extraordinary coincidence, that both Mr. Winston Churchill and Mr. Winston Churchill should insert a short note in their respective publications explaining to the public which are the works of Mr. Winston Churchill and which those of Mr. Winston Churchill. The text of this note might form a subject for future discussion if Mr. Winston Churchill agrees with Mr. Winston Churchill's proposition. He takes this occasion of complimenting Mr. Winston Churchill upon the style and success of his works, which are always brought to his notice whether in magazine or book form, and he trusts that Mr. Winston Churchill has derived equal pleasure from any work of his that may have attracted his attention.

In 1959 Bertrand Russell and Lord Russell of Liverpool wrote a joint letter to the *Times*:

"Sir: In order to discourage confusions which have been constantly occurring, we beg herewith to state that neither of us is the other."

• • •

BETTER SAFE

For several years during the Cold War, New York police guarded the Soviet consulate at 9 East 91st Street in Manhattan. Officers manned a pale blue guard post 24 hours a day. "It's like being a prisoner of war stuck in a telephone booth," one said.

The Soviets left in 1980, and the police department accordingly canceled the guard, but two months later the 23rd precinct received a call from an Officer Cowans who said that Inspector

Whitmore of police intelligence had ordered the guard to be re-activated. So the police resumed their vigil over the now-disused building.

Five months later, in May 1982, the police happened to mention the consulate duty in a report. "What booth?" asked a bewildered intelligence official. It turned out that Officer Cowans and Inspector Whitmore did not exist; the police had been guarding an empty building around the clock for five months, right through Christmas, for no reason.

They closed up shop and removed the booth. "Whoever did this was someone who wanted to break chops or who stood to gain from it," Lt. Robert McEntire told the *New York Times.* "We're not sure which, and we probably never will be."

· · ·

ANTHROPOLOGY

"Man is a biped without feathers."—Plato

"Drinking when we are not thirsty and making love all year round, madam; that is all there is to distinguish us from other animals."
—Pierre Beaumarchais

"Man is the only animal that can remain on friendly terms with the victims he intends to eat until he eats them."
—Samuel Butler

"Man is the only animal that laughs and weeps, for he is the only animal that is struck with the difference between what things are and what they ought to be." —William Hazlitt

"*Homo sapiens* is the species that invents symbols in which to invest passion and authority, then forgets that symbols are inventions."—Joyce Carol Oates

• • •

TUG OF WAR

Let's play a game. We'll take turns bidding for a dollar bill. Both of us will have to pay our final bids, and the winner gets to keep the dollar.

Not surprisingly, the bidding will soon reach 99 cents. But then I'll bid $1.00, giving up any hope of profit but getting at least the dollar for my trouble. And then you'll bid $1.01, with the same idea. And so on indefinitely: First we were bidding for gain, but now we're trying to minimize our losses.

It sounds absurd, but this game has led people to pay $5 for a $1 bill. Yale economist Martin Shubik invented it to show how an irrational decision can be reached by perfectly rational steps.

• • •

WIRE WORK

In 1897, con artist Soapy Smith opened a telegraph office in Skagway, Alaska. For five dollars, new arrivals in the Klondike Gold Rush could send 10 words to loved ones anywhere in the world, informing them of their safe arrival and imminent riches.

No one noticed that the cable was simply nailed to the back

of the building, and that its other end disappeared in the waters of Skagway Bay.

Telegraph lines did not reach Skagway until 1901.

• • •

A SIDE MATTER

Inscribe a pentagon in a unit circle:

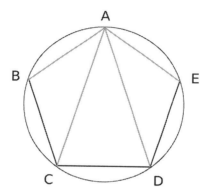

Now AB × AC × AD × AE = 5.

Pleasingly, this works with any regular *n*-gon: A hexagon yields 6, a heptagon 7, and so on.

• • •

HAPPENSTANCE

As the *Mayflower* was crossing the Atlantic in 1620, passenger John Howland was swept overboard during a storm. He managed to seize a trailing halyard and was pulled back to safety. His descendants in the New World have included:

- Franklin Roosevelt
- George H.W. Bush and George W. Bush
- Ralph Waldo Emerson
- Henry Wadsworth Longfellow
- Joseph Smith and Brigham Young
- Humphrey Bogart
- Benjamin Spock
- Sarah Palin
- Chevy Chase
- Christopher Lloyd
- Alec Baldwin

If Howland had lost his life in that storm, none of these people would have existed.

• • •

UNQUOTE

"God is a Republican, and Santa Claus is a Democrat."

—H.L. Mencken

• • •

COMPOUND INTEREST

On Jan. 18, 1897, California farmer George Jones bought a quantity of livestock feed from Henry B. Stuart of San Jose. As security he signed a $100 promissory note that bore 10 percent interest per month, compounded monthly.

They had agreed that Jones would pay the debt in three months, but the note had run for almost 25 years when Stuart got tired of waiting and told his lawyer to sue. Judge J.R. Welch of the Superior Court of Santa Clara entered this judgment on March 6, 1922:

"Wherefore, by virtue of the law and the facts, it is Ordered, Adjudged and Decreed that said Plaintiff have and recover from said Defendant the sum of $304,840,332,912,685.16 with interest thereon at the rate of 7% per annum until paid, together with the further sum of $50.00 Plaintiff's attorney's fees herein with interest thereon at the rate of 7% per annum until paid."

That's $304 trillion, "more money than there is in the world, outside of Russia," the *New York Tribune* reported drily. Jones paid $19.69 and filed for bankruptcy.

• • •

THE SHARK ARM AFFAIR

On April 25, 1935, a shark in Australia's Coogee Aquarium disgorged a human arm. The shark had recently been caught off Sydney, but no swimmers had been reported missing. The arm, which had been severed with a knife, was eventually identified as that of 40-year-old ex-boxer James Smith, who had been missing since April 7.

Police began a murder investigation, but without a body there was no proof that Smith was dead. The case collapsed, and it remains unsolved.

• • •

DOUBLE-BOOKED

In 1975, Émile Ajar won the Prix Goncourt for his novel *The Life Before Us*. The French literary prize is awarded only once to each author, so Ajar could not be recognized again.

Or so you'd think. It turned out that Ajar was a pen name of Romain Gary, who had already won the prize in 1956.

Gary/Ajar remains the only author to win the medal twice.

• • •

THE EDITORIAL LASH

Thomas Jefferson writhed under the criticisms of the Continental Congress as it reviewed his draft of the Declaration of Independence. Seeing this, Benjamin Franklin took him aside. "I have made it a rule," he said, "whenever in my power, to avoid becoming the draftsman of papers to be reviewed by a public body. I took my lesson from an incident which I will relate to you.

"When I was a journeyman printer, one of my companions, an apprenticed hatter, having served out his time, was about to open shop for himself. His first concern was to have a handsome signboard, with a proper inscription. He composed it in these words: *John Thompson, Hatter, makes and sells hats for ready money*, with a figure of a hat subjoined. But he thought he would submit it to his friends for their amendments.

"The first he showed it to thought the word *hatter* tautologous, because followed by the words *makes hats*, which showed he was a hatter. It was struck out. The next observed that the word *makes* might as well be omitted, because his customers would not care who made the hats; if good and to their mind they would buy, by whomsoever made. He struck it out. A third said he thought the words *for ready money* were useless, as it was not the custom of the place to sell on credit. Every one who purchased expected to pay. They were parted with, and the inscription now stood, *John Thompson sells hats*. 'Sells hats?' says his next friend; 'why, nobody will expect you to give them away.

What, then, is the use of that word?' It was stricken out, and *hats* followed, the rather as there was one painted on the board.

"So his inscription was ultimately reduced to *John Thompson,* with the figure of a hat subjoined."

• • •

A BAD WEEK

On Aug. 6, 1945, Mitsubishi engineer Tsutomu Yamaguchi was in Hiroshima visiting the company shipyard when the *Enola Gay*'s atomic bomb exploded overhead.

Badly burned, he spent the night in an air raid shelter and then returned to his hometown.

He was explaining the ordeal to his supervisor there when "at that moment, outside the window, I saw another flash and the whole office, everything in it, was blown over."

He lived in Nagasaki.

• • •

"A SATISFACTORY EXPLANATION"

" One of the curiosities some time since shown at a public exhibition, professed to be a skull of Oliver Cromwell. A gentleman present observed that it could not be Cromwell's, as he had a very large head, and this was a small skull. 'Oh, I know all that,' said the exhibitor, undisturbed, 'but, you see, this was his skull when he was a boy.'

— Ainsworth Rand Spofford, *The Library of Wit and Humor, Prose and Poetry,* 1894

• • •

FOOD DRIVE

Of sweetness, Shakespeare wrote: "A little more than a little is by much too much." Boston learned this the hard way in the Molasses Disaster of 1919, when someone tried to fill a weak tank with 2.3 million gallons of the thick syrup.

"A muffled roar burst suddenly upon the air," wrote the *Boston Herald*. "Mingled with the roar was the clangor of steel against steel and the clash of rending wood."

The tank collapsed, sending a giant wave of molasses sweeping through the North End. Even in the January cold, the wave would have been 8 to 15 feet high and traveled at 35 mph. It broke the girders of the elevated railway, lifted a train off its tracks, and tore a firehouse from its foundation. Twenty-one people stickily drowned, and 150 were injured. Cleanup took six months; one victim wasn't found for 11 days.

No one knows the cause, but it's been noted that molasses was used in making liquor, and the disaster occurred one day before

Prohibition was ratified. It appears the owners were trying to distill molasses into grain alcohol before the market dried up. Write your own pun.

• • •

HAPPY CRABBING!

On Feb. 5, 1958, during a simulated combat mission near Savannah, Ga., a B-47 bomber collided with an F-86 fighter. The fighter crashed; the bomber, barely airworthy, needed to reduce weight to avoid an emergency landing.

So it dropped a 7,600-pound nuclear bomb.

The bomb contained 400 pounds of conventional explosives and highly enriched uranium. There's some disagreement as to whether it included the plutonium capsule needed to start a nuclear reaction.

That's rather important, because in 50 years of searching the Air Force still hasn't found the bomb. It hit the water near Tybee Island off the Georgia coast and is presumably buried in 10 feet of silt somewhere in Wassaw Sound. But exactly where it is, and how dangerous it is, remain unknown.

• • •

STUBBORN

Write down any natural number, reverse its digits to form a new number, and add the two:

$$871$$
$$\underline{178}$$
$$1049$$

In most cases, repeating this procedure eventually yields a palindrome:

$$1049$$
$$\underline{9401}$$
$$10450$$

$$10450$$
$$\underline{05401}$$
$$15851$$

With 196, perversely, it does not—or, at least, it hasn't in computer trials, which have repeated the process until it produced numbers 300 million digits long.

Is 196 somehow immune to producing palindromes? No one's yet offered a conclusive proof—so we don't know.

• • •

IN A WORD

balatronic
adj. pertaining to buffoons

engastration
n. the act of stuffing one bird into another

impervestigable
adj. incapable of being fully investigated

antithalian
adj. opposed to fun

• • •

TRIVIUM

The state nearest Africa is Maine.

• • •

THE STARS ALIGN

It's only a happy accident that our moon "fits" over the sun's disc during a solar eclipse. The sun is 400 times the diameter of the moon, but it's nearly 400 times farther from Earth, so to us the two have almost exactly the same angular size.

• • •

SELF-HELP

In 1921, Pennsylvania surgeon Evan O'Neill Kane removed his own appendix. He wanted to show that a local anesthetic would be adequate for some surgeries but needed to be sure that a patient could tolerate the procedure. So on Feb. 15, propped up by pillows on an operating table, he cut into his own abdomen, using novocaine to dull the pain while a nurse held his head forward so that he could see the work.

"Just say that I am getting along all right," he told the *New York Times* the following day. "I now know exactly how the patient feels when being operated upon under local treatment. . . .I have demonstrated the fact in my own case that a major operation can be performed by the use of a local anesthesia without causing pain more severe than can be borne by the patient."

He was 60 years old at the time. Nine years later he would repair his own hernia.

• • •

QUICK THINKING

" 'It wasn't so very late, only a quarter of twelve.'

'How dare you sit there and and tell me that lie? I was awake when you came in, and looked at my watch, it was three o'clock.'

'Well, arn't three a quarter of twelve?'

— James Baird McClure, ed., *Entertaining Anecdotes From Every Available Source*, 1879

• • •

A MARINE DOPPELGANGER

On April 6, 1823, HMS *Leven* was surveying East Africa when she spied her consort, the *Barracouta*, about two miles to leeward. This was surprising, as the brig's sailing orders should have placed her far from that location, but *Leven*'s crew recognized her peculiar rig and the faces of her men. Strangely, she stood away when Captain Owen attempted to close with her, and near sunset she lowered a boat, apparently to pick up a man overboard.

The next morning the *Leven* anchored at Simon's Bay, and a full week passed before the *Barracouta* joined her there. Her log showed she had been 300 miles away when the *Leven* thought she saw her.

So what had the *Leven* seen? No other vessel of the *Barracouta*'s class had been seen about the Cape at that time. The sighting has never been explained.

• • •

BACON TESTIMONY

" Among trials of individual animals for special acts of turpitude, one of the most amusing was that of a sow and her six young ones, at Lavegny, in 1457, on a charge of their having murdered and partly eaten a child. . . .The sow was found guilty and condemned to death; but the pigs were acquitted on account of their youth, the bad example of their mother, and the absence of direct proof as to their having been concerned in the eating of the child.

— Robert Chambers, *The Book of Days*, 1864

• • •

ONE, THREE, FIVE. . .

In English, every odd number contains the letter E.

...

THE DYATLOV PASS INCIDENT

In February 1959, a search was organized when nine Russian ski hikers failed to return from a trek in the northern Ural Mountains. After six days, their abandoned camp was found in a mountain pass.

All the hikers were dead. Two were found on the opposite side of the pass, near the remains of a fire; three others had died closer to camp, apparently trying to return; and the remaining four were found only three months later, under 4 meters of snow in a nearby stream valley.

Apparently the victims had fled the tent suddenly on the night of Feb. 2, tearing their way out from the inside and running down the mountain. Though the temperature had been around -25° C, all were inadequately dressed, some wearing only underwear. Though the bodies had no external wounds, one showed severe skull damage and two had major chest fractures. One woman's tongue was missing.

In the end, Soviet investigators could conclude only that a "compelling natural force" had caused the hikers' deaths. That's all we know.

...

RIGHT OF WAY

" A Moral Principle met a Material Interest on a bridge wide enough for but one.

'Down, you base thing!' thundered the Moral Principle, 'and let me pass over you!'

The Material Interest merely looked in the other's eyes without saying anything.

'Ah,' said the Moral Principle, hesitatingly, 'let us draw lots to see which shall retire till the other has crossed.'

The Material Interest maintained an unbroken silence and an unwavering stare.

'In order to avoid a conflict,' the Moral Principle resumed, somewhat uneasily, 'I shall myself lie down and let you walk over me.'

Then the Material Interest found a tongue, and by a strange coincidence it was its own tongue. 'I don't think you are very good walking,' it said. 'I am a little particular about what I have underfoot. Suppose you get off into the water.'

It occurred that way.

— Ambrose Bierce, *Fantastic Fables*, 1898

• • •

ENFANT TERRIBLE

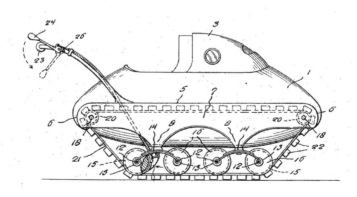

Anthony Peronti wasn't messing around when he designed this baby carriage, a sheet-metal torpedo with welded fenders and a tanklike tread:

With the above described construction I have provided a baby carriage which will move easily and quietly over any type of surface and by virtue of the flexibility of the springs, curbstones, door-steps and other minor obstacles can be negotiated without tilting the body of the carriage and with a minimum of jarring or discomfort to the passenger.

He filed the patent in November 1945, so perhaps he'd been inspired by the battlefield.

• • •

KAPREKAR'S CONSTANT

Choose four distinct digits and arrange them into the largest and smallest numbers possible (e.g., 9751 and 1579). Subtract the smaller from the larger to produce a new number (9751 − 1579 = 8172) and repeat the operation.

Within seven iterations you'll always arrive at 6174.

With three-digit numbers you'll aways arrive at 495.

• • •

GOING TO TOWN

 A fine tortoiseshell cat was on Friday morning the 27th ult. seen approaching London Bridge, peaceably seated in a large bowl-dish. As she advanced towards the fall, every one present anticipated that she would be overturned, and precipitated into the stream. She kept her seat, however, with great presence of mind, and amidst loud cheers shot the centre arch with as much dexterity as the most experienced waterman. A boy hearing her voice shortly after she had made the hazardous attempt, and fancying she wanted a pilot, rowed towards her, and took her into his wherry, when he found around her neck a parchment scroll, stating that she had come from Richmond Bridge, and directing, if she should reach London in safety, that she should be conveyed to a Mrs. Clarke, in High-street, in the Borough, who would reward the bringer. The boy, in pursuance of these instructions, conveyed poor puss to Mrs. Clarke, who seemed to be apprised of the circumstance, and rewarded the messenger with half a crown. It turned out that the voyage was undertaken for a wager between two Richmond Gentlemen, and that puss embarked at the turn of the tide in the course of the night, and happily reached her destination without sustaining any injury.

— *Caledonian Mercury*, Sept. 2, 1813

• • •

SHELL GAME

In the 1920s, American painter and eccentric Waldo Peirce gave a turtle to the concierge of the building in which he lived. She was delighted with the gift and took great care of her new pet, and she did not notice when Peirce secretly replaced it with a slightly larger turtle. This continued for some time, with Peirce sneaking successively larger turtles into her apartment while she praised her miraculous pet to the neighbors.

Then, after a suitable pause, he began using smaller turtles.

• • •

ALACKE, WHAT NOYSE IS THIS?

WILLIAM SHAKESPEARE is an anagram of I AM A WEAK-ISH SPELLER.

• • •

LIMERICK

There once was an old man of Lyme
Who married three wives at a time
When asked, "Why a third?"
He replied, "One's absurd
And bigamy, sir, is a crime."

— William Cosmo Monkhouse

• • •

AND MANY MORE

In 1891, Robert Louis Stevenson received a letter from a Vermont girl named Annie Ide. Her birthday fell on Christmas, she said, and she seldom received birthday presents.

He replied with a document decreeing that "I, Robert Louis Stevenson, . . .in consideration that Miss Annie H. Ide, . . .was born, out of all reason, upon Christmas Day, and is therefore out of all justice denied the consolation and profit of a proper birthday; and considering that I, the said Robert Louis Stevenson, have attained an age when we never mention it, and that I have now no further use for a birthday of any description. . . . HAVE TRANSFERRED, and DO HEREBY TRANSFER, to the said Annie H. Ide, ALL AND WHOLE my rights and privileges in the thirteenth day of November, formerly my birthday, now, hereby, and henceforth, the birthday of the said Annie H. Ide, to have, hold, exercise, and enjoy the same in the customary manner, by the sporting of fine raiment, eating of rich meats, and receipt of gifts, compliments, and copies of verse, according to the manner of our ancestors."

He charged her to add "Louisa" to her name, "at least in private," and to use the birthday "with moderation and humanity"—and he directed that if she neglected these conditions the birthday would revert to the president of the United States. She didn't.

• • •

UNQUOTE

"We have not the reverent feeling for the rainbow that a savage has, because we know how it is made. We have lost as much as we gained by prying into that matter."

—Mark Twain

"At last I fell fast asleep on the grass & awoke with a chorus of birds singing around me, & squirrels running up the trees & some Woodpeckers laughing, & it was as pleasant a rural scene as ever I saw, & I did not care one penny how any of the beasts or birds had been formed."

—Charles Darwin, letter to his wife, April 28, 1858

ANSWERS *and* SOLUTIONS

AN ALARMING PARADOX (PAGE 9)

The "three travellers" are Francis Drake, Thomas Cavendish, and William Dampier, each of whom circled the globe. On such a journey, your head does indeed travel farther than your feet— about 37 feet farther, if you're 6 feet tall and the globe is a perfect sphere.

• • •

A RIDDLE (PAGE 16)

The whip.

• • •

CLUTCH CARGO (PAGE 23)

Call a person an Odd if he has shaken hands an odd number of times (at any given moment). An Even has shaken hands an even number of times.

At the start, the number of Odds is zero, an even number. As the evening progresses, three types of handshake take place:

- An Odd shakes with an Odd. In this case they both become Evens; the total number of Odds decreases by 2.
- An Even shakes with an Even. Both become Odds, and the number of Odds increases by 2.

- An Even shakes with an Odd. The Even becomes an Odd, and the Odd becomes an Even, so the total number of Odds remains unchanged.

Because the number of Odds can change only by an even number, the number of people who have shaken hands an odd number of times remains even—not only at the end of the evening, but at every moment throughout!

• • •

C STORY (PAGE 41)

It's a bit worse than you thought. You'll type for 300 quintillion years before reaching ONE OCTILLION.

Stupid demons.

• • •

"WHO CAN TELL?" (PAGE 47)

Letters.

• • •

THE LOCK KEY (PAGE 50)

None. The same amount of water is necessary to raise any boat.

One way to make this intuitive is to imagine that a 2-meter "slab" of water is inserted at the *bottom* of the lock chamber. This will raise a boat of any size to the level of the higher lake.

• • •

A HIKING PUZZLE (PAGE 58)

The simplest solution is to imagine that the man's twin climbs the mountain while he himself descends it.

Clearly the two will meet at the same point, and at the same time.

• • •

HEADS OF STATE (PAGE 74)

Zero. If nine receive their own hats, then the tenth must as well.

• • •

ONE OF A KIND (PAGE 87)

The chance of rolling no sixes is

$$5/6 \times 5/6 \times 5/6 \times 5/6 \times 5/6$$

The chance of rolling exactly one six is

$$1/6 \times 5/6 \times 5/6 \times 5/6 \times 5/6$$

. . .times 5, because the six can appear on any one of the five dice. So the probabilities are equal.

• • •

ROUND TRIP (PAGE 102)

He's anywhere within 10 miles of the South Pole, where these directions take him across the pole ("10 miles in a straight line") and back again.

• • •

A MARTIAN CENSUS (PAGE 105)

The key is that the number of fingers can tell us uniquely the number of Martians. That's a tall order. It eliminates, say, 246 fingers, because that's too ambiguous: There might be 82 Martians with 3 fingers each, or 3 Martians with 82 fingers each, and so on. The only possibility that avoids this uncertainty is that the quantity of Martians and the quantity of fingers per Martian are expressed by the same number, and that this number is not composite. That means we're looking for the square of a prime number, and the only such number in the range 200-300 is 289, or 17^2. So there are 17 Martians, each of which has 17 fingers. This is the only number between 200 and 300 that permits such a definite assertion.

• • •

VARYING REPORTS (PAGE 116)

The statements contradict one another, so only one can be true. That means nine are false, so statement 9 is true.

• • •

THE STOPPED CLOCK (PAGE 123)

Before she leaves the house, Andrea winds her own clock and sets it to an arbitrary time. Then she notes the correct time at her friend's house both when she arrives and when she leaves. When she returns home she consults her own clock to see how much time the whole trip has taken, subtracts the period she spent at her friend's house, and divides the result by two to learn the travel time in each direction. By adding this interval to the time she noted as she left her friend's house, she can infer the current time and set her own clock.

• • •

TEMPTING (PAGE 125)

No, you shouldn't accept. Surprisingly, the odds of receiving such a hand are 1,827 to 1, overwhelmingly favoring the earl.

It's said that Charles Anderson Worsley (1809-1897), the second Earl of Yarborough, made a considerable amount of money offering this challenge to whist players. Even today such a hand in bridge is known as a Yarborough.

• • •

WHAT IS IT? (PAGE 131)

The letter H.

In 1850 Horace Mayhew composed a Cockney rejoinder:

> I dwells in the Hearth, and I breathes in the Hair;
> If you searches the Hocean you'll find that I'm there.
> The first of all Hangels in Holympus am Hi,
> Yet I'm banished from 'Eaven, expelled from on 'igh.
> But, though on this Horb I'm destined to grovel,
> I'm ne'er seen in an 'Ouse, in an 'Ut, nor an 'Ovel.
> Not an 'Orse nor an 'Unter e'er bears me, alas!
> But often I'm found on the top of a Hass.
> I resides in a Hattic, and loves not to roam,
> And yet I'm invariably absent from 'Ome.
> Though 'Ushed in the 'Urricane, of the Hatmosphere part,
> I enters no 'Ed, I creeps into no 'Art.

Only look, and you'll see in the Heye Hi appear;
Only 'Ark, and you'll 'Ear me just breathe in the Hear.
Though in sex not an 'E, I am (strange paradox)
Not a bit of an 'Effer, but partly a Hox.
Of Heternity I'm the beginning! and, mark,
Though I goes not with Noar, I'm first in the Hark.
I'm never in 'Ealth, have with Fysic no power,
I dies in a month, but comes back in a Hour.

• • •

BLOCKED (PAGE 144)

Let x be the number of blocks in a full row. Then

$$n = x^3 - x$$

$$= x(x + 1)(x - 1).$$

These factors are three consecutive integers, which means that at least one of them is even and one is divisible by 3.

Since its factors include numbers that are divisible by both 2 and 3, n is divisible by 6.

• • •

ROCK AND ROLL (PAGE 148)

The slab will have moved forward 2 meters, not 1. If the slab were removed, 1 turn would advance the rollers 1 meter. If the rollers were held in place, 1 turn would advance the slab 1 meter. Combining the two motions means that 1 turn advances the slab 2 meters.

• • •

LIGHT WORK (PAGE 152)

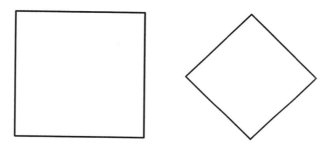

• • •

BREAKING BAD (PAGE 160)

Amy will win. Each move increases the number of pieces by one, so each of Amy's moves yields an even number of pieces. Because there are 48 squares altogether, she will make the last move.

• • •

THE POTATO PARADOX (PAGE 178)

Perhaps surprisingly, the potatoes now weigh 50 pounds. The sack of potatoes originally weighed 100 pounds, and 1 percent of its weight, or 1 pound, was non-water. If that 1 pound now makes up 2 percent of the total weight, then the total weight is 50 pounds.

Not a paradox, exactly, but many people find it counterintuitive.

• • •

GENDER ISSUES (PAGE 181)

The first set of births after the sultan's decree will be half boys and half girls. But so will every subsequent set. The number of births will diminish steadily, but this won't affect the ratio of boys to girls.

• • •

BREAD ALONE (PAGE 188)

Assume each of the eight loaves was divided into 3 pieces, making 24 altogether.

Andy's 5 loaves made 15 pieces. He ate 8 and gave the remaining 7 to Carl.

Bill's 3 loaves made 9 pieces. He ate 8 and gave the remaining 1 to Carl.

So Andy should get 7 gold pieces and Bill 1.

• • •

HOPE AND CHANGE (PAGE 190)

There's actually no difficulty here. The desk clerk has $25, the guests have $3, and the bellboy has $2.

The "trouble" arises only because we're trying to add the bellboy's $2 to the guests' $27. Instead we should subtract it, giving $25 for the clerk, which is correct.

In effect, the men paid $27 for a $25 room, and the clerk gave the change to the bellboy.

INDEX

Aaron, Hank, co-authoring
  baseballs, 155
actors, unemployed, cross-
  dressing, 121
Adams, Franklin Pierce, 176
Ade, George, 171
airships, and pussycats, 19
Ajar, Émile, 205
algebra, and Lewis Carroll, 51
altitude, of showoff vultures,
  118
amnesia, whopping, 14
Andrea Doria "miracle girl," 95
Andrée, S.A., indomitability of,
  87
animal trials, 213
animals, observing religion, 15
antipodes, namesakes, 86
Apollo 11 and baseball, 161
apples
  difficult to sell, 26
  poetically sized, 99
approbation, by the Texas legis-
  lature, of serial murder, 80
Arecibo observatory, and
  breakfast foods, 159
Armand-Delille, Paul, rabbit
  murderer, 64

arms, disgorged by Australian
  sharks, 205
assassinations, assiduous
  attendance at, 76
at that game, two, playing, 20
aurora borealis
  emulated artificially, 89
  powering telegraphs, 152
automobiles, complexity not a
  virtue of, 41
awards, literary, collected by
  doppelgängers, 205

Babbage, Charles, fact-checking
  Tennyson, 172
babies, and crocodiles, 24
baby carriages, armored, 215
balloons, using, to explore
  arctic, don't, 87
bank runs, slower than horses,
  141
Barham, battleship, 50
Barrymore, Ethel, airily
  parented, 188
baseball
  and mathematics, 155
  and moon landings, 161
Bastille, difficult to lock, 172

Made in the USA
Middletown, DE
21 December 2018